COMMON CORE

MATH

Activities that Captivate, Motivate & Reinforce

Grade 3

by Marjorie Frank

Incentive Publications
World Book, Inc.
a Scott Fetzer company

Illustrated by Kathleen Bullock
Cover by Penny Laporte
Edited by Joy MacKenzie

ISBN 978-0-86530-739-1

World Book, Inc.
233 North Michigan Avenue
Suite 2000
Chicago, Illinois, 60601 U.S.A.

For information about other World Book publications, visit our website at
www.worldbook.com or call **1-800-967-5325**.

Printed in the United States by Sheridan Books, Inc.
Chelsea, Michigan
2nd Printing December 2013

CONTENTS

Number and Operations in Base Ten

Number and Operations—Fractions

Measurement and Data

Geometry

Assessment & Answer Keys

Great Support for
Common Core Standards!

Invite your students to join in mysteries and adventures with colorful characters! They will delight in the high-appeal topics and engaging visuals. They can

   . . . watch frog races, skydiving competitions, and turtle hurdle events;

   . . . solve problems about hula hoops, trampolines, and skateboards;

   . . . figure out the source of creepy noises in the woods;

   . . . face an underwater scuba diving challenge;

   . . . take part in a subtraction snowball fight;

   . . . visit dance contests and bug races;

   . . . tackle math questions in a swamp or at a picnic;

   . . . determine the fate of injured skiers;

   . . . enjoy tales of wild bull-riding;

   . . . and tackle many other delightful tasks.

And while they engage in these ventures, they will be moving toward competence with critical math skills, processes, and standards that they need for success in the real world.

How to Use this Book

- The pages are tools to support your teaching of the concepts, processes, and skills outlined in the Common Core State Standards. This is not a curriculum; it is a collection of engaging experiences for you to use as you do math with your children or students.

- Use any given page to introduce, explain, teach, practice, extend, assess, provide independent work, start a discussion about, or get students collaborating on a skill or concept.

- Use any page in a large group or small group setting to deepen understandings and expand knowledge or skill.

- Each activity is focused on a particular standard, but most make use of or can be expanded to strengthen other standards as well.

- The book is organized according to the Common Core math domains. Use the tables on pages 9–16 and label at the bottom corner of each activity page to identify the standard category supported by each page.

- Use the labels on the Contents pages to see specific standards/skills for each page.

- For further mastery of Common Core State Standards, use the suggestions on the next page (page 8).

About Common Core Math Standards

The Common Core State Math Standards seek to expand conceptual understanding of the key ideas of math while they strengthen foundational skills, operations, and principles. They identify what students should know, understand, and be able to do—with an emphasis on explaining principles and applying them to a wide range of situations. To best help students gain and master these robust standards for math . . .

1. Know the standards well. Keep them in front of you. Understand for yourself the big picture of what the standards seek to do. (See www.corestandards.org.)

2. Work to apply, expand, and deepen student skills. With activities in this book (or any learning activities), plan to include

   . . . interaction with peers in pairs, small groups, and large groups

   . . . plenty of discussion, integration, and hands-on work with math concepts

   . . . emphasis on questioning, analyzing, modeling math situations, explaining what you are doing and thinking, using tools effectively, and applying to real world problems

   . . . lots of observation, meaningful feedback, follow-up, and reflection

3. Ask questions that advance reasoning, application, and real-life connection:

- *What, exactly, IS the problem?*
- *Can you solve this another way?*
- *Does this make sense? (Why or why not?)*
- *Can you state the problem in a different way?*
- *What information is needed to solve this problem?*
- *What information in the problem is not needed?*
- *What operations do you need to use?*
- *If we change ____, what will happen to ____?*
- *What tools do you need to solve this?*
- *Can you draw your problem-solving process?*
- *What did you learn from solving this problem?*
- *When could you use this? Where could you use this?*
- *Now that you know how to ____, where can you use this?*

- *How did you arrive at your answer?*
- *How can you show that your answer is right?*
- *Where else have you seen a problem like this?*
- *What does this ask you to do?*
- *What led you to this conclusion?*
- *How could we figure this out?*
- *What was the first step you took?*
- *What information is missing?*
- *How could you make a model of this?*
- *How could you draw your solution?*
- *How do you know this is right?*
- *What patterns do you notice?*
- *Where have you seen this in real life?*
- *What does this remind you of?*
- *Could there be another answer?*
- *If this is true, what else might be true?*
- *How can you explain your answer?*
- *Could you ask that question differently?*
- *What will you do next?*

Standards for Mathematical Practice, Grades K-12

St. #	Standard	Pages in This Book
1	Make sense of problems and persevere in solving them.	18–126
2	Reason abstractly and quantitatively.	18–29, 31, 32, 35–42, 44–58, 60–68, 75–78
3	Construct viable arguments and critique the reasoning of others.	Applicable to all pages
4	Model with mathematics.	65–78, 90–110, 112–124
5	Use appropriate tools strategically.	80–11
6	Attend to precision.	18–126
7	Look for and make use of structure.	18–32, 41, 42, 57, 58, 90–110
8	Look for and express regularity in repeated reasoning.	30, 41, 42, 57, 58, 90–98, 112–124

Grade 3 Common Core State Standards for Mathematical Content

3.OA   Operations and Algebraic Thinking

St. #	Standard	Pages in This Book
	Represent and solve problems involving multiplication and division.	
1	Interpret products of whole numbers (e.g.: interpret 5 x 7 as the total number of objects in 5 groups of 7 objects each or 7 groups of 5 objects each).	18, 19, 20, 21, 22, 23, 25, 27, 28, 29
2	Interpret whole-number quotients of whole numbers (e.g. 56 ÷ 8 as the total number of objects in each share when 56 objects are partitioned equally into 8 shares or as a number of shares when 56 objects are partitioned into equal shares of 8 objects each).	21, 22, 23, 24, 25, 27, 28, 29
3	Use multiplication and division within 100 to solve word problems in situations involving equal groups, arrays, and measurement quantities e.g. by using drawings and equations with a symbol for the unknown number to represent the problem.	18, 19, 20, 21, 22, 23, 24, 25, 26, 27, 28, 29, 30, 31, 32
4	Determine the unknown whole number in a multiplication or division equation relating three whole numbers.	18, 19, 20, 21, 22, 23, 24, 25, 27, 28, 29, 30, 31, 32
	Understand properties of multiplication and the relationship between multiplication and division.	
5	Apply properties of operations as strategies to multiply and divide. Commutative property of multiplication, Associative property of multiplication, Distributive property.	18, 19, 21, 22, 23, 25, 28, 30, 31, 32
6	Understand division as an unknown-factor problem.	21, 23, 24, 27, 28, 29, 31, 32

3.OA   Operations and Algebraic Thinking, continued

St. #	Standard	Pages in This Book
	Multiply and divide within 100.	
7	Fluently multiply and divide within 100 using strategies such as the relationship between multiplication and division or properties of operations. By the end of Grade 3, know from memory all products of two one-digit numbers.	18, 19, 20, 21, 22, 23, 24, 25, 26, 27, 28, 29, 30, 31, 32, 33, 34, 35, 36, 37, 39, 40, 41, 42
	Solve problems involving the four operations, and identify and explain patterns in arithmetic.	
8	Solve two-step word problems using the four operations. Represent these problems using equations with a letter standing for the unknown quantity. Assess the reasonableness of answers using mental computation and estimation strategies including rounding.	35, 36, 37, 38, 39, 40, 41, 42 add
9	Identify arithmetic patterns (including patterns in the addition table or multiplication table) and explain them using properties of operations.	30, 41, 42

Grade 3 Common Core State Standards for Mathematical Content

3.NBT   Number and Operations in Base Ten

St. #	Standard	Pages in This Book
	Use place value understanding and properties of operations to perform multi-digit arithmetic.	
1	Use place value understanding to round whole numbers to the nearest 10 or 100.	44, 45, 46, 47, 48, 49
2	Fluently add and subtract within 1000 using strategies and algorithms based on place value, properties of operations, and/or the relationship between addition and subtraction.	50, 51, 52, 53, 54, 55, 56
3	Multiply one-digit whole numbers by multiples of 10 in the range 10–90 (e.g., 9 × 80, 5 × 60) using strategies based on place value and properties of operations.	41, 42, 57, 58

Grade 3 Common Core State Standards for Mathematical Content

3.NF   Number and Operations—Fractions

St. #	Standard	Pages in This Book
Develop understanding of fractions as numbers.		
1	Understand a fraction 1/b as the quantity formed by 1 part when a whole is partitioned into *b* equal parts; understand a fraction *a/b* as the quantity formed by *a* parts of size 1/*b*.	60, 61, 62, 63, 64
2	Understand a fraction as a number on the number line; represent fractions on a number line diagram.	
2a	Represent a fraction 1/b on a number line diagram by defining the interval from 0 to 1 as the whole and partitioning it into *b* equal parts. Recognize that each part has size 1/*b* and that the endpoint of the part based at 0 locates the number 1/*b* on the number line.	65, 66, 67
2b	Represent a fraction *a/b* on a number line diagram by marking off *a* lengths 1/*b* from 0. Recognize that the resulting interval has size *a/b* and that its endpoint locates the number *a/b* on the number line.	65, 66, 67
3	Explain equivalence of fractions in special cases, and compare fractions by reasoning about their size.	
3a	Understand two fractions as equivalent (equal) if they are the same size, or the same point on a number line.	68, 69
3b	Recognize and generate simple equivalent fractions, (e.g., 1/2 = 2/4, 4/6 = 2/3). Explain why the fractions are equivalent, e.g., by using a visual fraction model.	68, 69, 70, 71, 72, 75
3c	Express whole numbers as fractions, and recognize fractions that are equivalent to whole numbers. *Examples: Express 3 in the form 3 = 3/1; recognize that 6/1 = 6; locate 4/4 and 1 at the same point of a number line diagram.*	73, 74, 75
3d	Compare two fractions with the same numerator or the same denominator by reasoning about their size. Recognize that comparisons are valid only when the two fractions refer to the same whole. Record the results of comparisons with the symbols >, =, or <, and justify the conclusions, e.g., by using a visual fraction model.	76, 77, 78

3.MD   Measurement and Data

St. #	Standard	Pages in This Book
	Solve problems involving measurement and estimation of intervals of time, liquid volumes, and masses of objects.	
1	Tell and write time to the nearest minute and measure time intervals in minutes. Solve word problems involving addition and subtraction of time intervals in minutes, e.g., by representing the problem on a number line diagram.	80, 81, 82, 83
2	Measure and estimate liquid volumes and masses of objects using standard units of grams (g), kilograms (kg), and liters. Add, subtract, multiply, or divide to solve one-step word problems involving masses or volumes that are given in the same units, e.g., by using drawings (such as a beaker with a measurement scale) to represent the problem.	84, 85, 86, 87, 88, 89
	Represent and interpret data.	
3	Draw a scaled picture graph and a scaled bar graph to represent a data set with several categories. Solve one- and two-step "how many more" and "how many less" problems using information presented in scaled bar graphs.	90, 91, 92, 93
4	Generate measurement data by measuring lengths using rulers marked with halves and fourths of an inch. Show the data by making a line plot, where the horizontal scale is marked off in appropriate units—whole numbers, halves, or quarters.	94, 95, 96, 97, 98
	Geometric measurement: understand concepts of area and relate area to multiplication and to addition.	
5	Recognize area as an attribute of plane figures and understand concepts of area measurement.	
5a	A square with side length 1 unit, called "a unit square," is said to have "one square unit" of area, and can be used to measure area.	100, 101
5b	A plane figure which can be covered without gaps or overlaps by n unit squares is said to have an area of n square units.	100, 101

3.MD Measurement and Data, continued

St. #	Standard	Pages in This Book
	Geometric measurement: understand concepts of area and relate area to multiplication and to addition . . . (continued)	
6	Measure areas by counting unit squares (square cm, square m, square in, square ft, and improvised units).	99, 100–101, 102, 105, 106
7	Relate area to the operations of multiplication and addition.	99, 100–101, 102, 105, 106
7a	Find the area of a rectangle with whole-number side lengths by tiling it, and show that the area is the same as would be found by multiplying the side lengths.	99, 100–101, 102, 105, 106
7b	Multiply side lengths to find areas of rectangles with whole number side lengths in the context of solving real world and mathematical problems, and represent whole-number products as rectangular areas in mathematical reasoning.	99, 100–101, 102, 105, 106
7c	Use tiling to show in a concrete case that the area of a rectangle with whole-number side lengths a and $b + c$ is the sum of $a \times b$ and $a \times c$. Use area models to represent the distributive property in mathematical reasoning.	105
7d	Recognize area as additive. Find areas of rectilinear figures by decomposing them into non-overlapping rectangles and adding the areas of the non-overlapping parts, applying this technique to solve real world problems.	99, 100–101, 102, 105, 106
	Geometric measurement: recognize perimeter as an attribute of plane figures and distinguish between linear and area measures.	
8	Solve real world and mathematical problems involving perimeters of polygons, including finding the perimeter given the side lengths, finding an unknown side length, and exhibiting rectangles with the same perimeter and different areas or with the same area and different perimeters.	103, 104, 107, 108, 109, 110

3.G   Geometry

St. #	Standard	Pages in This Book
Reason with shapes and their attributes.		
1	Understand that shapes in different categories (e.g., rhombuses, rectangles, and others) may share attributes (e.g., having four sides), and that the shared attributes can define a larger category (e.g., quadrilaterals). Recognize rhombuses, rectangles, and squares as examples of quadrilaterals, and draw examples of quadrilaterals that do not belong to any of these subcategories.	112, 113, 114, 115, 116, 117, 118, 119, 120, 121, 122, 123
2	Partition shapes into parts with equal areas. Express the area of each part as a unit fraction of the whole.	124, 125, 126

Copyright © Incentive Publications
Common Core Reinforcement Activities — 3rd Grade Math

OPERATIONS
AND
ALGEBRAIC
THINKING

Grade 3

Underwater Search

Follow the directions at the bottom to color things under the sea.

Use the picture to solve the problems on the next page (page 19).

Color the sharks purple.   Color the turtles green.

Color the seahorse orange.

Color the small fish yellow.   Color the starfish blue.

Color the treasure chests brown.

Color the crabs red.   Color the shells pink.

Color each octopus gray.

Use with page 19.

Name

Represent, Solve x and ÷

Underwater Search, continued

Follow the directions for problems 1–9.

Circle groups of things on page 18.

Fill in each box with the missing number.

1. Circle ⬜ groups of 2 = 4

2. Circle ⬜ groups of 1 = 2

3. Circle 3 groups of ⬜ = 3

4. Circle 2 groups of ⬜ = 6

5. Circle 3 groups of ⬜ = 3

 6. Circle ⬜ groups of 1 = 2

7. Circle ⬜ group of 5 = ⬜

8. Circle 5 groups of ⬜ = 10

9. Circle ⬜ group of 1 = 1

Use with page 18.

Name

Represent, Solve x and ÷

Who Wins the Race?

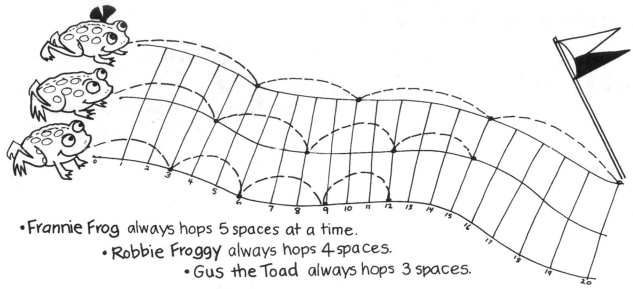

- Frannie Frog always hops 5 spaces at a time.
  - Robbie Froggy always hops 4 spaces.
    - Gus the Toad always hops 3 spaces.

In this race they each hop 4 times, so Frannie wins the race.

Tell who will win each of the races below.

Race 1
Frannie	3 hops x 5 spaces =
Robbie	4 hops x 4 spaces =
Gus	6 hops x 3 spaces =

Who wins? _____

Race 2
Frannie	6 hops x 5 spaces =
Robbie	6 hops x 4 spaces =
Gus	3 hops x 3 spaces =

Who wins? _____

Race 3
Frannie	2 hops x 5 spaces =
Robbie	3 hops x 4 spaces =
Gus	4 hops x 3 spaces =

Who wins? _____

Race 4
Frannie	3 hops x 5 spaces =
Robbie	1 hops x 4 spaces =
Gus	2 hops x 3 spaces =

Who wins? _____

Race 5
Frannie	5 hops x 5 spaces =
Robbie	4 hops x 4 spaces =
Gus	3 hops x 3 spaces =

Who wins? _____

Race 6
Frannie	2 hops x 5 spaces =
Robbie	3 hops x 4 spaces =
Gus	2 hops x 3 spaces =

Who wins? _____

Name _____

How Many Jumps?

This hurdler jumps 9 spaces with each jump.

He starts at the beginning of the number line and finishes 45 spaces later at the finish line.

He must jump 5 times to get the end.

We can write this problem.

45 spaces ÷ 5 jumps = 9 spaces per jump

Practice these facts.

1. 56 ÷ 7 jumps = ☐ per jump

2. 72 ÷ 8 jumps = ☐ per jump

3. ☐ ÷ 3 jumps = 9 per jump

4. ☐ ÷ 4 jumps = 4 per jump

5. 81 ÷ ☐ jumps = 9 per jump

6. 40 ÷ ☐ jumps = 5 per jump

7. 20 ÷ 5 jumps = ☐ per jump

8. 27 ÷ 3 jumps = ☐ per jump

9. 64 ÷ ☐ jumps = 8 per jump

10. 15 ÷ ☐ jumps = 3 per jump

11. ☐ ÷ 3 jumps = 4 per jump

12. ☐ ÷ 7 jumps = 7 per jump

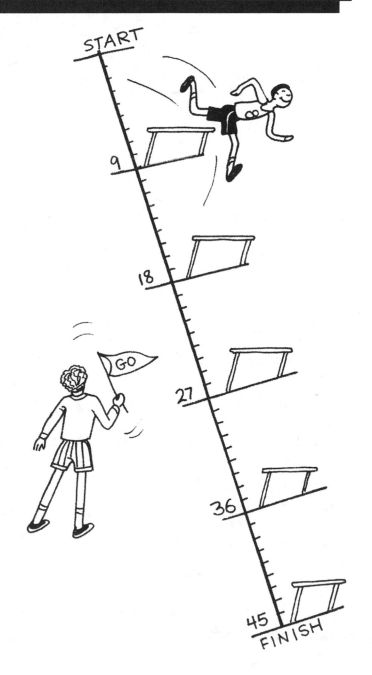

Name

Common Core Reinforcement Activities — 3rd Grade Math   **Represent, Solve x and ÷**

Numbers from the Sky

The sky is filled with numbers. Find a number on a parachute to solve each problem. Color each parachute as you use the number.

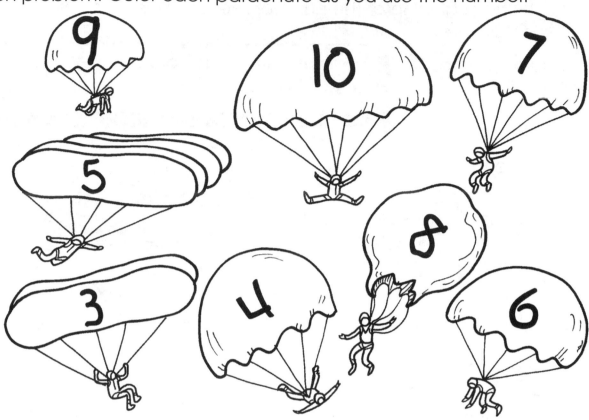

1. J.J. jumped 72 times. He jumped 8 times each week. How many weeks did he jump? _____

2. Belle drank 3 quarts of water after each jump. She drank 27 quarts. How many times did she jump? _____

3. Mike has taken a total of 25 jumps. He uses a parachute for 5 jumps, then gets a new one. How many parachutes has he used? _____

4. Lucia has spent 66 dollars on her jumps. Each jump costs 11 dollars. How many times has she jumped? _____

5. Teri eats the same number of cupcakes after each jump. So far he has eaten 30 cupcakes. He has jumped 10 times. How many cupcakes does he eat each time? _____

6. Ryan jumped the same number of times every month for 6 months. He jumped a total of 48 times. How many times did he jump each month?

_____

Name

Watch Out!

Yikes! This scuba diver is surrounded by stinging jellyfish. How many are in each group?

Look at each group of jellyfish. Fill in the missing numbers below the group.

1.

4 x ☐ = ☐

2.

☐ x 5 = ☐

3.

☐ x 2 = ☐

4.

3 x ☐ = ☐

Gack!

5.

☐ x ☐ = ☐

6.

☐ x ☐ = ☐

Represent, Solve x and ÷

Meet the Athletes

Read the name, age, and sport of each athlete.

Answer the questions and fill in the missing numbers.

Emma (72) skydiver

George (88) weightlifter

Jean (20) diver

Abby (3) gymnast

Chen (50) unicycler

Benjy (10) boxer

Rick (18) dancer

Suzy (11) pole-vaulter

Tammy (40) biker

Roberto (9) surfer

1. Which athlete is 6 times Abby's age?_____

   ☐ x 6 = ☐

2. The athlete whose age is
   Emma's age divided by 8 is a _____ .

   ☐ ÷ 8 = ☐

3. Which athlete is 5 times the boxer's age?_____

   ☐ x 5 = ☐

4. Which athlete is the biker's age divided by 2? _____

   ☐ ÷ 2 = ☐

5. Which athlete is 8 times the age of the pole-vaulter? _____

   8 x ☐ = ☐

Name _____

Hula Hoop Questions

Jessie and her friends can spin hula hoops a long time without dropping them!

Fill in the missing number in each hula hoop.

Jan
4 spins a second
for 6 seconds =
_____ total spins

June
3 spins a second
for 9 seconds =
_____ total spins

Julie
10 spins
a second for
10 seconds =
_____
total spins

Jamie
4 spins a second
for _____ seconds =
32 total spins

Janet
_____ spins a second
for 6 seconds =
54 total spins

James
_____ spins a second
for 7 seconds =
42 total spins

Jerri
_____ spins a second
for 6 seconds =
48 total spins

Jenny
7 spins a second
for _____ seconds =
63 total spins

John
_____ spins a second
for 9 seconds =
45 total spins

Justin
5 spins a second
for _____ seconds =
25 total spins

Name _____

Represent, Solve x and ÷

Bouncing Problems

There is a whole lot of bouncing going on!

Find the missing number with each clue.

Write the numbers into the puzzle.

ACROSS

1. 6 x 8 = ____
4. 1000 x 2 = ____
5. 210 x 2 = ____
7. 7 x 8 = ____
8. 8 x 5 = ____
9. 101 x 3 = ____
11. 7 x 5 = ____
13. 10 x 5 = ____
14. 8 x 4 = ____
16. 5 x 6 = ____
17. 9 x 8 = ____

DOWN

1. 111 x 4 = ____
2. 6 x 1000 = ____
3. 5 x 1111 = ____
4. 100 x 2 = ____
6. 4 x 6 = ____
9. 3 x 100 = ____
10. 9 x 4 = ____
11. 3 x 111 = ____
12. 7 x 111 = ____
13. 100 x 5 = ____
15. 3 x 9 = ____

Name

Represent, Solve x and ÷

26

Busy Feet

Athletes wear many different kinds of footwear.
Each of these pieces of footwear has a question for you.
The answer is the number described by the clues. Write each number.

10 miles a day
for 9 days

1. How many miles
have I run?

_____ miles

81 jumps
9 each day

2. How many days
have I jumped? *

_____ days

3 goals a game
for 6 games

3. How many goals
have I scored?

_____ goals

20 points
a game
for a
total of
200 points

4. How many games
have I played?

_____ games

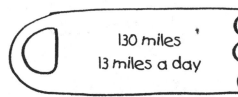
130 miles
13 miles a day

5. How many days
have I swum?

_____ days

9 lifts a day
for 9 days

6. How many ski lifts
have I ridden?

_____ lifts

36 stolen bases
6 a game

7. How many
games?

_____ games

1 game a day
for 1000 days

8. How many games
have I bowled?

_____ games

7 dances a month
total 63 dances

9. How many months
have I performed?

_____ months

Name _____

Represent, Solve x and ÷

Lost in the Cave

A spelunker is someone who explores caves.

These spelunkers are looking for lost signs to put into the number sentences.

Find the right sign for each sentence. Each sign can be used many times.

1. 4 ☐ 7 = 28
2. 3 ☐ 2 = 6
3. 8 ☐ 5 = 40
4. 5 ☐ 3 = 15
5. 6 ☐ 2 = 3

11. 9 ☐ 1 = 9
12. 10 ☐ 2 = 5
13. 5 ☐ 9 = 45
14. 9 ☐ 6 = 54
15. 3 ☐ 3 = 9

6. 4 ☐ 4 = 1
7. 3 ☐ 8 = 24
8. 7 ☐ 8 = 56
9. 14 ☐ 2 = 7
10. 90 ☐ 1 = 90

16. 80 ☐ 10 = 8
17. 5 ☐ 0 = 0
18. 20 ☐ 1 = 20
19. 6 ☐ 6 = 1
20. 10 ☐ 5 = 2

Name

Hide and Seek

Chester is playing hide and seek. He is looking for missing numbers.

In each number sentence, **n** stands for the missing number.

Find the number for **n**. Write it in the box.

You can use a number more than once. Color the numbers after you use them.

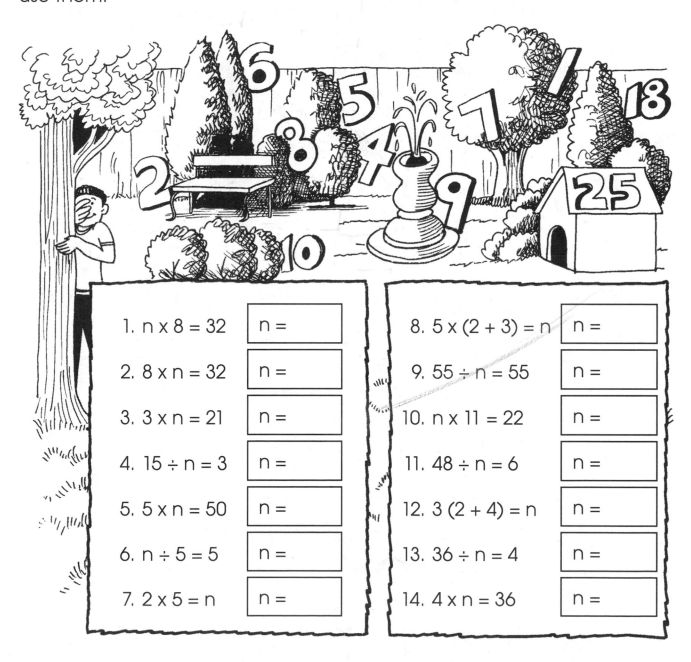

1. n x 8 = 32   n =

2. 8 x n = 32   n =

3. 3 x n = 21   n =

4. 15 ÷ n = 3   n =

5. 5 x n = 50   n =

6. n ÷ 5 = 5   n =

7. 2 x 5 = n   n =

8. 5 x (2 + 3) = n   n =

9. 55 ÷ n = 55   n =

10. n x 11 = 22   n =

11. 48 ÷ n = 6   n =

12. 3 (2 + 4) = n   n =

13. 36 ÷ n = 4   n =

14. 4 x n = 36   n =

Name

Properties, Relationships x and ÷

Patterns on the Bench

Some members of the softball team are waiting on the bench.
The numbers on their shirts follow a pattern. What is it?

The pattern is +3 to each shirt. The next number will be 24.

Finish the pattern, write the missing numbers on the shirts.
Be ready to explain the pattern.

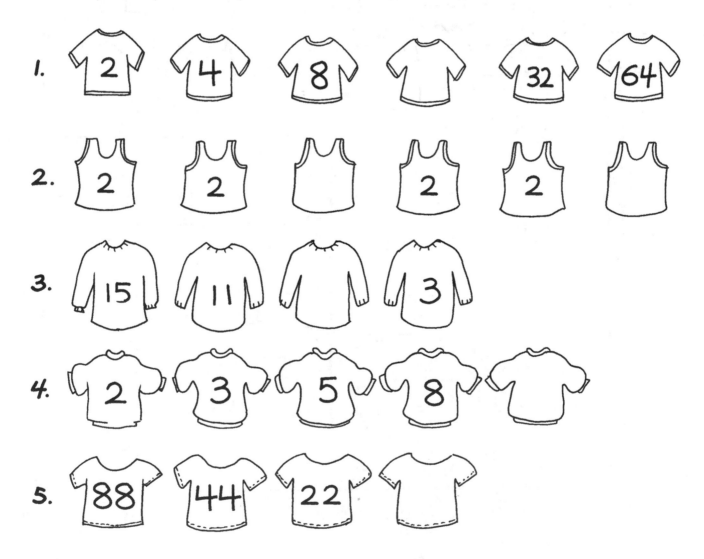

1. 2   4   8   ___   32   64

2. 2   2   ___   2   2   ___

3. 15   11   ___   3

4. 2   3   5   8   ___

5. 88   44   22   ___

Name

Skateboard Tricks

If you are good with multiplication facts, division is as easy as riding a skateboard. You just need to know the trick!

In a division problem, look for the missing factor.

Find the missing factor in the box below the skater.
Then follow the directions for coloring the skateboards.

1.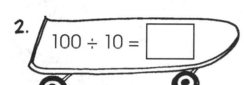
$72 \div \boxed{} = 8$

2.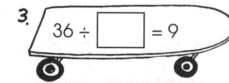
$100 \div 10 = \boxed{}$

3.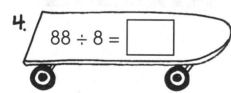
$36 \div \boxed{} = 9$

4.
$88 \div 8 = \boxed{}$

5.
$35 \div 5 = \boxed{}$

6.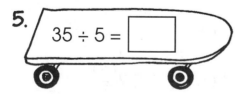
$63 \div 7 = \boxed{}$

7.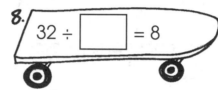
$18 \div \boxed{} = 3$

8.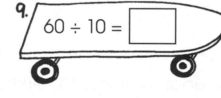
$32 \div \boxed{} = 8$

9.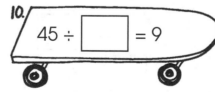
$60 \div 10 = \boxed{}$

10.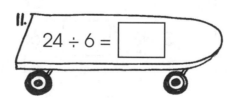
$45 \div \boxed{} = 9$

11.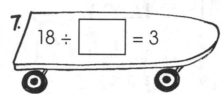
$24 \div 6 = \boxed{}$

12.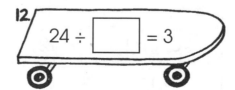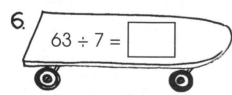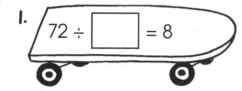
$24 \div \boxed{} = 3$

Look for the missing factor. Write it in the problem. Then decorate the skateboard with the color shown.

6   purple
8   red
10   orange
5   green
9   yellow
4   silver
7   blue
11   gold

Name

Properties, Relationships x and ÷

Sports Runs in the Family

The Morris family is a family of sports lovers.

The problems below each show a fact family.

Multiplication and division facts come in families.

> 4, 6, and 24 are all in a family because
>
> 4 x 6 = 24   24 ÷ 4 = 6
> 6 x 4 = 24   24 ÷ 6 = 4

Fill in the missing fact in each of these families.

1. 6 x 2 = ☐

   12 ÷ 2 = ☐

2. 4 x 9 = ☐

   36 ÷ 4 = ☐

3. ☐ x 5 = 45

   ☐ ÷ 5 = 9

4. 9 x 6 = ☐

   ☐ ÷ 6 = 9

5. 48 ÷ ☐ = 6

   ☐ x 8 = 48

6. 3 x ☐ = 12

   12 ÷ 4 = ☐

7. 20 ÷ 5 = ☐

   4 x 5 = ☐

8. 7 x 7 = ☐

   49 ÷ ☐ = 7

9. 11 x ☐ = 121

   121 ÷ 11 = ☐

Name

Mystery Athlete

Who is the mystery athlete? Solve the problems to find out!

Use the KEY to find the letters that match each answer.

Write the letters in the spaces at the bottom of the page.

1. 123
   x 8

2. 334
   x 4

3. 156
   x 7

4. 109
   x 9

5. 361
   x 6

6. 816
   x 2

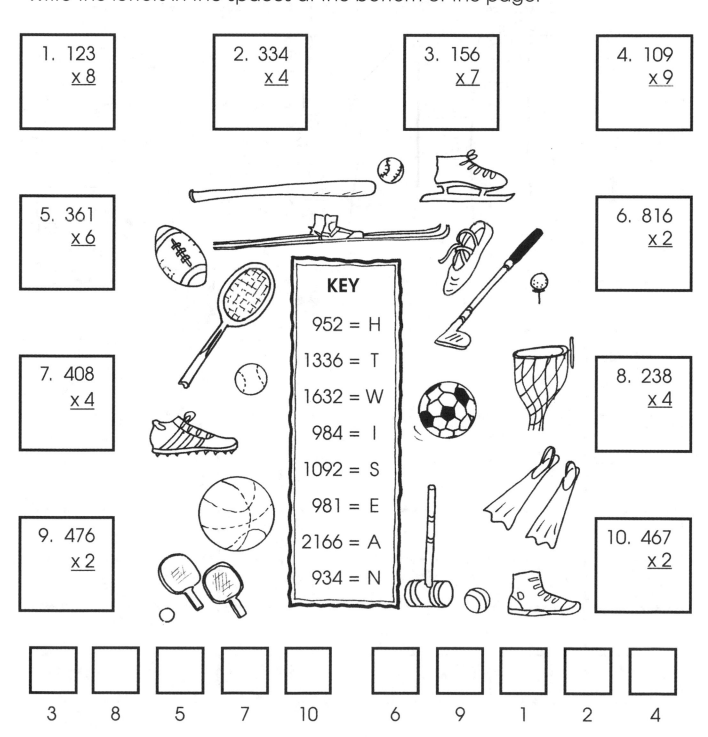

KEY

952 = H

1336 = T

1632 = W

984 = I

1092 = S

981 = E

2166 = A

934 = N

7. 408
   x 4

8. 238
   x 4

9. 476
   x 2

10. 467
    x 2

3   8   5   7   10   6   9   1   2   4

Name

Solve x and ÷ to 100

Is It Tic-Tac-Toe?

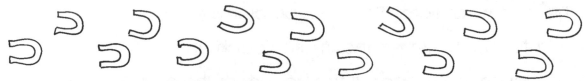

In each row across, one answer is different from the others.

Put a big, red **X** on the different answer.

To win, you must get a line of X's either across, up and down, or diagonally.

A.

2⟌22	6⟌66	9⟌90
8⟌72	4⟌32	4⟌36
7⟌77	3⟌30	8⟌80

Which games are winners? _____

Ladies and Gentlemen!
It's 'Tic-Tac-Toe' by a nose!

B.

4⟌24	6⟌54	9⟌54
2⟌44	7⟌49	3⟌66
7⟌56	5⟌20	6⟌48

C.

8⟌160	5⟌45	7⟌63
9⟌90	4⟌20	7⟌35
8⟌72	7⟌70	9⟌81

Name _____

Wild River Ride

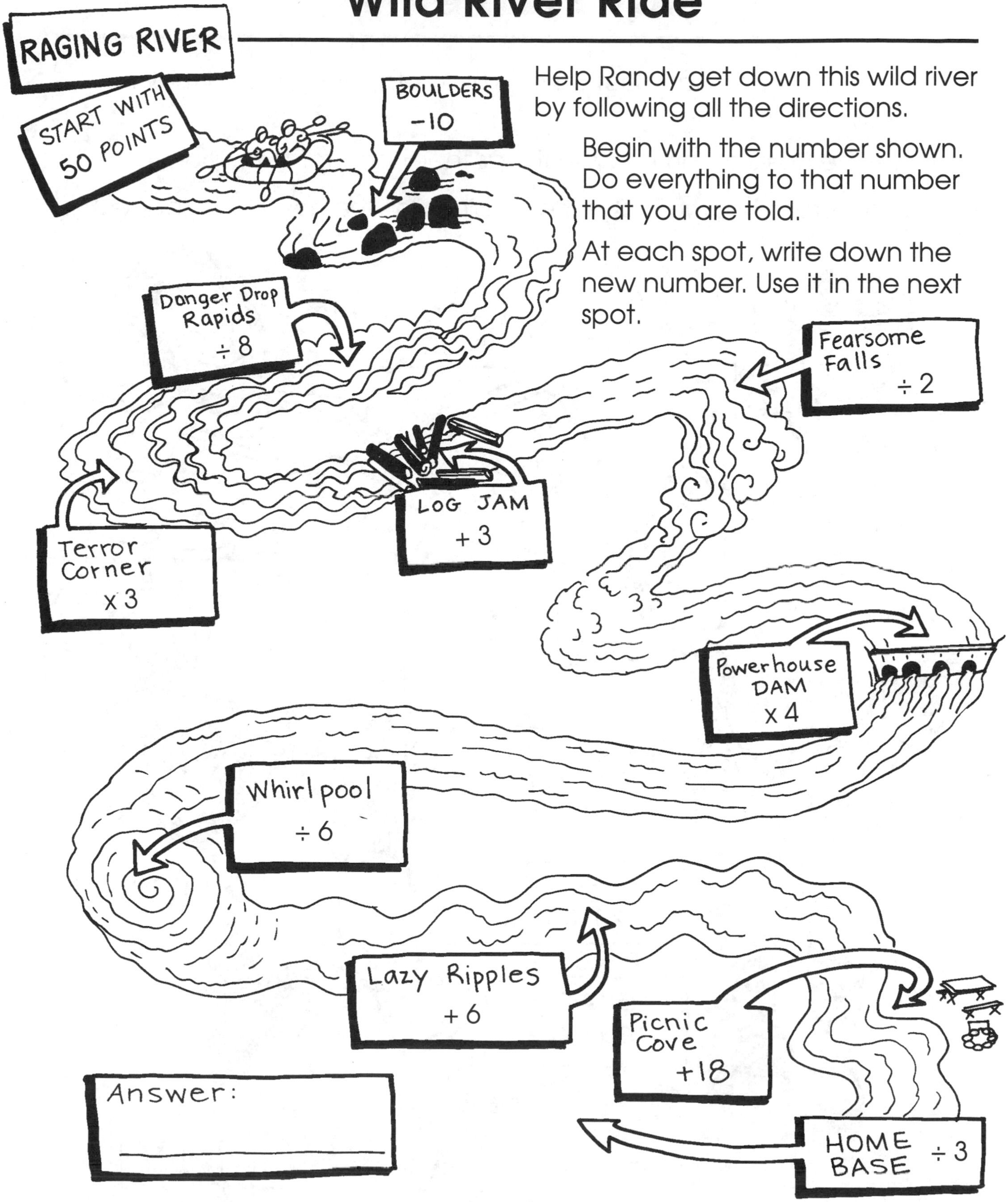

RAGING RIVER

START WITH 50 POINTS

BOULDERS
-10

Help Randy get down this wild river by following all the directions.

Begin with the number shown. Do everything to that number that you are told.

At each spot, write down the new number. Use it in the next spot.

Danger Drop Rapids
÷ 8

Fearsome Falls
÷ 2

LOG JAM
+ 3

Terror Corner
x 3

Powerhouse DAM
x 4

Whirlpool
÷ 6

Lazy Ripples
+ 6

Picnic Cove
+18

Answer:

HOME BASE ÷ 3

Name

Solve x and ÷ to 100

Icy Problems

Hannah and Harvey can't get on the ice to play hockey until they have all the right equipment.

Here are the costs of some of the things they need for their sport.

Use this picture to help you solve the problems on the next page (page 37).

HELMET $39.95

SHOULDER PADS $32.50

STICK $15.42

JERSEY $19.00

ELBOW PADS $14.99 pair

GLOVES $23.65

PANTS $69.98

KNEE GUARDS $29.25 pair

SKATES $100.00

PUCK $5.00

Use with page 37.

Name _____

Icy Problems, continued

Use the picture of the hockey players on page 36 to solve the problems.

1. How much did Hannah spend on her skates and her stick?

    $ 100.00
    + 15.42

2. Harvey had $50.00. He bought a helmet. How much change did he get?

    $ 50.00
    − 39.95

3. Which costs less, a jersey or a stick? _____

    How much less?

4. When Hannah bought her shoulder pads and elbow pads, she gave the clerk $50.00. Was that enough?

    _____

5. How much would 2 jerseys cost?

6. Which is more: elbow pads and a stick or knee guards?

    _____

7. $100.00 skates
      + 39.95 helmet

8. $19.00 jersey
      + 15.42 stick

9. $ 65.98 pants
      + 39.95 helmet

10.   Hannah bought 7 pucks. How much did she pay?

Use with page 36.

Name _____

Problems, Patterns: 4 operations

Meet Me at the Snack Bar

During the game, Tammy and Tracy work at the snack bar.
Help them make the correct change for each customer.

MENU

ICE CREAM . . . . $ .75
POPCORN . . . . $ .25
FRENCH FRIES $1.00
PIZZA $1.25
GUM . . . . $ .10
SODA POP . . . . $ .60
JUICE . . . . $ .85
MILKSHAKE $1.50

---

1. **Ice Cream**

You give $ 1.00

Cost   – _____

Change

2. **Pizza**

You give $ 2.00

Cost   – _____

Change

3. **2 packs of gum**

You give $ .50

Cost   – _____

Change

4. **Juice**

You give $ 1.00

Cost   – _____

Change

5. **Soda & French Fries**

You give $ 2.00

Cost   – _____

Change

6. **Milkshake**

You give $ 5.00

Cost   – _____

Change

7. **Popcorn**

You give $ .50

Cost   – _____

Change

8. **French Fries**

You give $ 5.00

Cost   – _____

Change

Name

Cheers for the Team

Every team needs fans! Sports wouldn't be as much fun without them. Solve these problems about the fans at the Championship Swim Meet.

1. 35 fans were cheering for the Dolphins. 46 fans cheered for the Sharks. How many fans were cheering?

_____

2. Carlos went to buy a snow cone from the snack bar. It cost 40¢. He had 25¢. How much more does he need?

_____

3. Anna's mom brought hats for all 7 people in their family. Anna and Danna dropped theirs under the bleachers. How many hats were left?

_____

4. The pool has 4 rows of bleachers with 12 spaces in each row. How many fans can fit in the bleachers?

_____

5. Lily watched the swimmers line up for the relay. There were 5 teams, each with 4 swimmers. How many swimmers are racing in all?

_____

6. Angie brought jelly beans for her friends in the stands. She has 100 to share among 3 friends and herself. How many jelly beans will each girl get?

_____

Name _____

Problems, Patterns: 4 operations

Tasty Problems

Look at all the food Gabe ate at the soccer game!
In problems 1 to 4, write an answer to the question.
Circle an answer for problems 5 to 8.

1.  The popcorn cost 2 dollars. Gabe bought 3 in the first half of the game and 2 in the second half of the game. How much did he spend?

$2 \times (3 + 2) = n$ What is **n**?_____

2.  Gabe bought 24 hot dogs. He shared them equally among some friends and himself. Each ate 6 dogs. How many people ate?

$6 \times n = 24$ What is **n**?_____

3.  The pizza had 16 slices. Gabe ate 2 and gave slices to his friends. There were 3 slices left. How many slices did his friends eat?

$(16 - 2) - n = 3$ What is **n**?_____

4.  Each basket of chips has 11 chips. Gabe bought 6 baskets. When he was tired of eating chips, there were 20 chips left. How many did he eat?

$(11 \times 6) - n = 20$ What is **n**?_____

Name

Lollipops cost 90 cents each.

5.  Gabe wanted four. He thought the lollipops would cost a total of 5 dollars.

Was he right?   yes   no

6.  Gabe found 29 soda cans. His friend Jana found 20. Jana said, "We need 51 more to have 100."

Was she right?   yes   no

7.  Each pack of gum had 5 sticks. Gabe wanted 2 sticks for each of his 10 friends.

Should he buy 8 packs of gum?
         yes   no

8.  An ice cream cone cost 3 dollars. Gabe had 19 dollars. He thought he could buy 15 cones.

Does that make sense?
         yes   no

The Big Race

These rowers are practicing for a big race. Solve some of their rowing problems.

In problems 1 to 5, write the answer to the question. Circle an answer for problem 6.

1. Abby rows 40 strokes a minute. Adam rows with her, but he rests 10 strokes out of each minute. How many strokes do they row together in one minute?

   $40 + (40 - 10) = n$

   What is **n**? _____

2. The rowing team crossed a 9-mile lake six times last week. Then they crossed another lake once. They rowed a total of 70 miles. How long was the second lake?

   $(9 \times 6) + n = 70$

   What is **n**? _____

3. When Adam and Abby row a mile, they each drink 2 quarts of water. They row 10 miles a day for 5 days. How much water do they drink?

   $2 \times (2 \times (10 \times 5))$

   What is **n**? _____

4. The team rowed
   6 miles on Monday
   12 miles on Tuesday
   18 miles on Wednesday
   24 miles on Thursday
   30 miles on Friday.

   What pattern do you see?

   _____

   _____

5. The team rowed
   3600 strokes the first hour
   3200 strokes the second hour
   2800 strokes the third hour
   2400 strokes the fourth hour

   What pattern do you see?

   _____

   _____

6. Adam and Abby thought they had rowed 10,000 strokes in ten minutes. Does this make sense?

   yes   no

Name

A Prize Fly Catcher

Grandpappy Bullfrog is a prize-winning fly catcher. He wins all the contests. Look at the chart of Grandpappy's scores from the latest contest.

Which number sentences about Grandpappy's scores are true?
Write T (for True) on the lines for the true sentences.

_____ 1. ST = SN + T

_____ 2. T + TH = TH + T

_____ 3. F – TH = 1000

_____ 4. W + F = F + W

_____ 5. T = ST – SN

_____ 6. TH ÷ 48 = 1000

_____ 7. W + TH < F

_____ 8. F ÷ 6 = 900

_____ 9. TH ÷ 6 = 900

_____ 10. M x 2 = ST

Write an answer for these

_____ 11. Every score can be divided evenly by each of these numbers: 2, 6, 10, and 100.

_____ 12. Every score can be divided evenly by each of these numbers: 6, 8, and 100.

13. What is the pattern of Grandpappy's scores from Sunday to Saturday?

_____

_____

_____

_____

Grandpappy's Scores
Swamptown Fly-Catching Contest, 2012

	Day	Number of Flies Caught
SN	Sunday	2,400
M	Monday	3,000
T	Tuesday	3,600
W	Wednesday	4,200
TH	Thursday	4,800
F	Friday	5,400
ST	Saturday	6,000

Name

Problems, Patterns: 4 operations

Copyright © Incentive Publications
Common Core Reinforcement Activities — 3rd Grade Math

NUMBER
AND
OPERATIONS
IN
BASE TEN

Grade 3

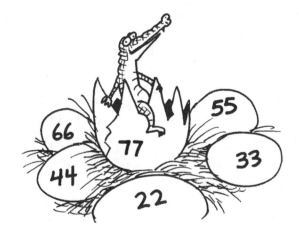

Snorkeling with Sam

Tootsie Turtle was invited to go snorkeling with Snorkel Sam.
See what they discover underwater in the Hokee Penokee Swamp!
Find the numbers of things they saw by using
the clues below.

1. Sam saw this many spoonbill catfish:

    ☐ ☐ ☐ ☐ *Clues:*
    - The 5 is in the ones place.
    - The 6 is in the tens place.
    - The 2 is in the hundreds place.
    - The 3 is in the thousands place.

2. Tootsie saw this many tiny snails:
    (Use 1, 2, 6, and 6.)

    ☐ ☐ ☐ ☐ *Clues:*
    - The greatest numbers are in the tens and thousands places.
    - The ones place has the smallest number.

3. Sam and Tootsie gawked at this many purple sunfish: (Use 3, 2, 5, and 9.)

    ☐ ☐ ☐ ☐ *Clues:*
    - The smallest number is in the thousands place.
    - The greatest number is in the ones place.
    - The 5 is in the tens place.

4. They blew this many air bubbles:
    (Use 5, 8, 0, and 4.)

    ☐ ☐ ☐ ☐ *Clues:*
    - The biggest number is in the thousands place.
    - An ODD number is in the ones place.
    - A 0 is in the hundreds place.

5. Sam and Tootsie gazed at this many yellow-bellied carp: (Use 7, 3, 6, and 2.)

    ☐ ☐ ☐ ☐ *Clues:*
    - The 7 is in the tens place.
    - The number in the thousands place is TWICE the number in the hundreds place.

6. They saw this many tadpoles:
    (Use 2, 4, 1, and 6.)

    ☐ ☐ ☐ ☐ *Clues:*
    - The largest number is in the thousands place.
    - The smallest number is in the ones place.
    - The number in the tens place is < the number in the hundreds place.

7. They saw this many crayfish:
    (Use 1, 0, 0, and 7.)

    ☐ ☐ ☐ ☐ *Clues:*
    - The second largest number is in the thousands place.
    - The largest number is in the tens place.

Name

Those Lazy Snakes

The Snake family would rather watch the races than compete in them!

They are sunning themselves on the banks of the swamp, waiting for the river race to begin.

Follow the directions to round the numbers on each sleeping snake.

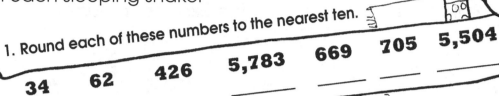

1. Round each of these numbers to the nearest ten.

34   62   426   5,783   669   705   5,504

2. Round each of these numbers to the nearest ten.

129   55   284   7,777   201   991   9,262

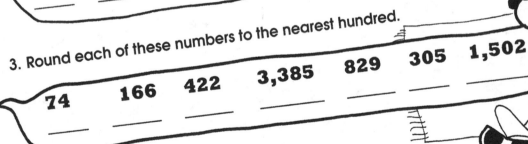

3. Round each of these numbers to the nearest hundred.

74   166   422   3,385   829   305   1,502

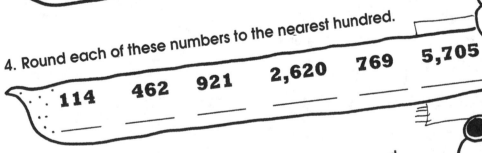

4. Round each of these numbers to the nearest hundred.

114   462   921   2,620   769   5,705

5. Round each of these numbers to the nearest thousand.

552   15,666   6,690   88,111

Name

Place Value, Rounding

Turtle Hurdles

The crickets need some hurdles for their track race.

They have decided to use the turtles for hurdles!

Help them finish the race by finishing the problems.

Below each turtle is a number written to show the place value of each digit.

Write a BIG numeral on the turtle to match the expanded number.

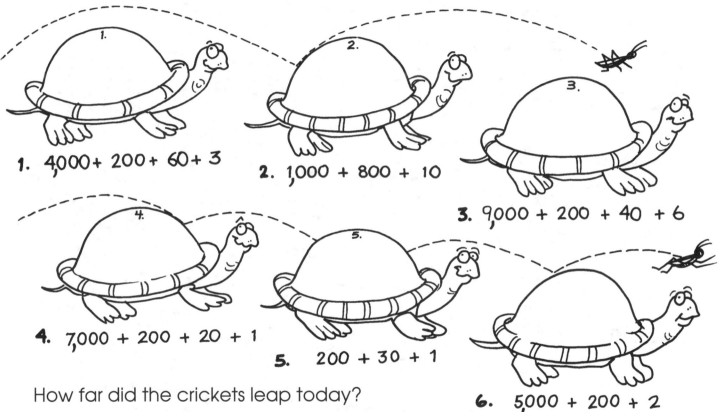

1. 4,000 + 200 + 60 + 3

2. 1,000 + 800 + 10

3. 9,000 + 200 + 40 + 6

4. 7,000 + 200 + 20 + 1

5. 200 + 30 + 1

6. 5,000 + 200 + 2

How far did the crickets leap today?

Write the expanded number on the line.

Sample: 6,294 feet = <u>6000 + 200 + 90 + 4</u>

7. Cissy Cricket hopped 329 feet = _____

8. Crusty Cricket hopped 678 feet = _____

9. Crabby Cricket hopped 590 feet = _____

10. Creaky Cricket hopped 1,572 feet = _____

11. Charlie Cricket hopped 4,477 feet = _____

12. Chirpy Cricket hopped 2,831 feet = _____

Name

Bubble-Blowing Bats

The Bat twins are blowing bubbles while they relax after flying practice. Oops! Some of the answers in the bubbles are WRONG.

Find the correct bubbles. Color them different colors. Do NOT color bubbles with wrong answers.

Take your pencil and "pop" the wrong ones.
Write the correct answer inside!

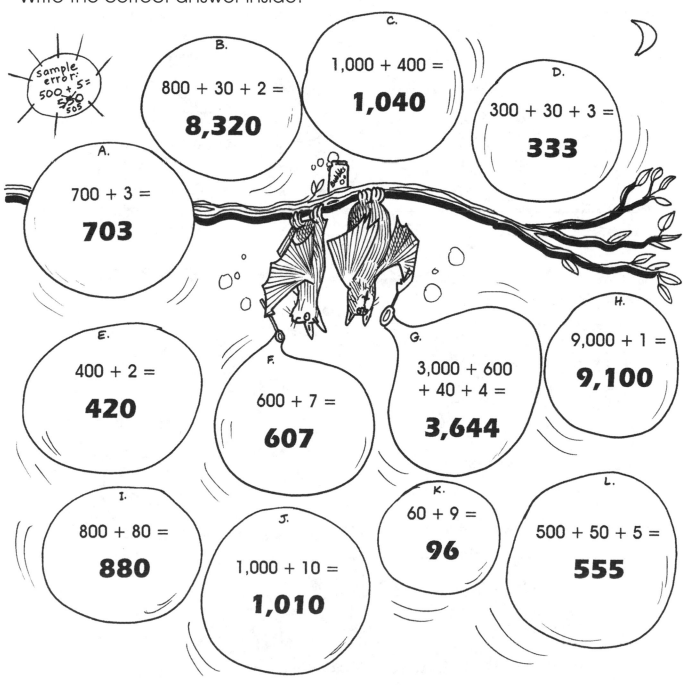

sample error:
500 + 5 =
505

B.
800 + 30 + 2 =
8,320

C.
1,000 + 400 =
1,040

D.
300 + 30 + 3 =
333

A.
700 + 3 =
703

E.
400 + 2 =
420

F.
600 + 7 =
607

G.
3,000 + 600 + 40 + 4 =
3,644

H.
9,000 + 1 =
9,100

I.
800 + 80 =
880

J.
1,000 + 10 =
1,010

K.
60 + 9 =
96

L.
500 + 50 + 5 =
555

Name

Place Value, Rounding

A Weighty Roundup

Wrestling is a popular sport in the Hokee Penokee Swamp.
The wrestlers always get weighed before every wrestling match.

Round the weight for each wrestler to the nearest TEN.
Write the rounded weight under each animal's name.

Bout No. 1:
Maniac Mouse   vs.   Big Al

1._____   2._____

Bout No. 2:
Slippery Sheila   vs.   Dinah the Destroyer

3._____   4._____

Bout No. 3:
Beetle Brain   vs.   Bug Eyes

5._____   6._____

Bout No. 4:
Ferocious Flamingo   vs.   Perilous Polly

7._____   8._____

Bout No. 5:
Big Bad Bosco   vs.   Sam the Squeeze

9._____   10._____

Name

Staying Cool

Staying cool on a hot, muggy swamp day is simply heavenly!
Flossy is not only cool. She is also feeling lazy.

Help her solve the number puzzle.
Read the clues.

Then write the correct numbers
in the right puzzle spaces.

CLUES

ACROSS
  A. 9 ones and 8 tens
  B. 7 hundreds, 4 tens, 6 ones
  E. 5 hundreds, 5 tens, 5 ones,
      3 thousands
  G. 2 ones and 4 thousands
  H. 5 thousands, 7 hundreds,
      3 tens, 6 ones
  J. 9 ones, 1 hundred, 2 thousands
  L. 8 hundreds, 9 thousands, 7 tens
  N. 3 tens, 5 ones, 1 hundred

DOWN
  A. 8 thousands, 6 hundreds,
      6 tens, 5 ones
  C. 3 tens, 2 ones, 6 thousands
  D. 90 thousands, 7 ones
  F. 5 thousands, 7 hundreds,
      2 ones
  I. 2 tens, 6 hundreds
  J. 2 thousands, 4 hundreds,
      8 tens, 3 ones
  K. 9 ones, 9 tens
  M. 7 tens, 7 thousands, 1 hundred
  N. 6 ones, 1 ten

Name

Place Value, Rounding

Lost in the Weeds

Michael has lost his sports equipment in the weeds. What is it?
Solve each addition problem. Find the answer in the code box.
Color each section with the color that matches the answer.

Code

36 = blue	84 = yellow
99 = green	62 = orange
70 = brown	100 = red
179 = purple	

What is the missing sports equipment?_____

Name _____

Catch Some Right Answers

This cowgirl is lassoing some addition and subtraction problems. She only wants to catch problems with right answers.

Which ones should she lasso?

Color lassos around problems with right answers.

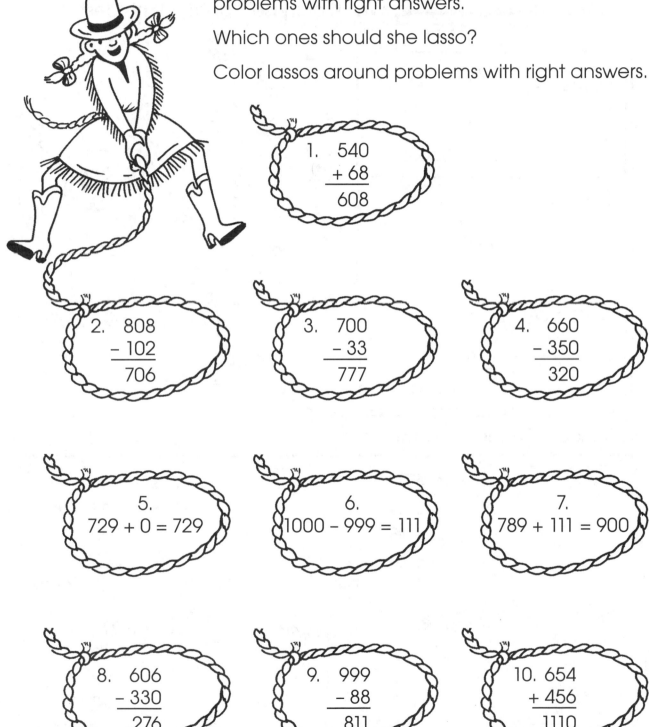

1. 540
    + 68
    608

2. 808
    – 102
    706

3. 700
    – 33
    777

4. 660
    – 350
    320

5.
729 + 0 = 729

6.
1000 – 999 = 111

7.
789 + 111 = 900

8. 606
    – 330
    276

9. 999
    – 88
    811

10. 654
    + 456
    1110

Name

+ and – within 1000

Throw Three!

In this dart game, Ramon gets to throw 3 darts in each game.
Add up his score for each game.

Which of these 3 games is his best? _____

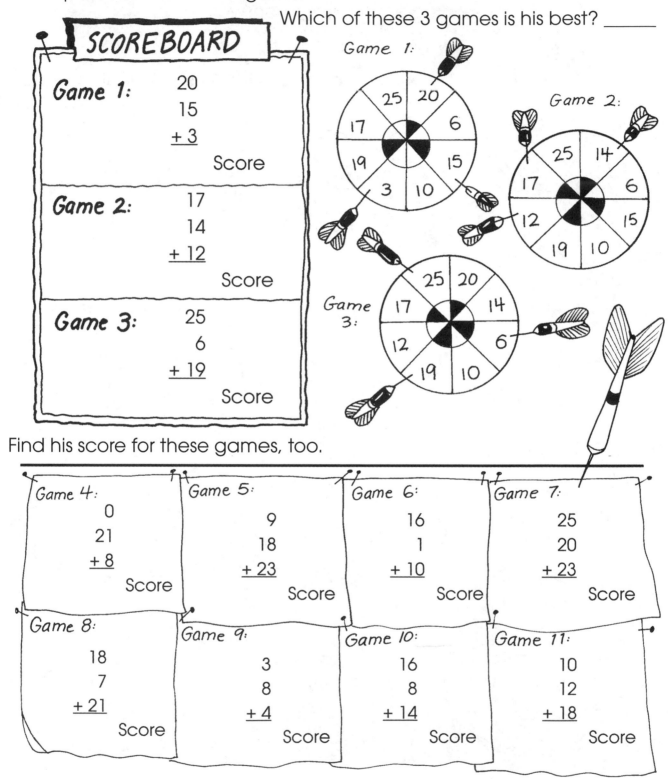

SCOREBOARD

Game 1:
  20
  15
  + 3
  Score

Game 2:
  17
  14
  + 12
  Score

Game 3:
  25
  6
  + 19
  Score

Find his score for these games, too.

Game 4:
  0
  21
  + 8
  Score

Game 5:
  9
  18
  + 23
  Score

Game 6:
  16
  1
  + 10
  Score

Game 7:
  25
  20
  + 23
  Score

Game 8:
  18
  7
  + 21
  Score

Game 9:
  3
  8
  + 4
  Score

Game 10:
  16
  8
  + 14
  Score

Game 11:
  10
  12
  + 18
  Score

Name

Surprising Sports Facts

When you solve these problems, you will get answers to some interesting sports facts. You might already know some of these facts. Others might surprise you!

1. 71
    − 49
    feet on a starting soccer team

2. 48
    − 39
    Olympic gold medals held by U.S. swimmer Mark Spitz

3. 99
    − 74
    age of the youngest world champion race-car driver

4. 1340
    +1151
    points scored by Michael Jordan in 1995-1996 season

5. 123
    −109
    age of the youngest women's world champion figure skater

6. 11
    + 15
    miles in a marathon

7. 760
    − 755
    rings in the Olympic symbol

8. 259
    −243
    balls in a billiard (pool) game

9. 156
    + 144
    yards in the length of a polo field

10. 850
    − 829
    points in a ping-pong match

11. 39
    + 15
    outs in a 9-inning baseball game

12. 92
    − 88
    riders on an Olympic bobsled

13. 263
    + 137
    dimples on a golf ball

Name _____

+ and − within 1000

Different Sails

Each sail has a different difference.

Solve the subtraction problem on each sail.

Color sails with answers > 100 **red**.

Color sails with answers < 50 **blue**.

Color sails with answers > 70 and < 100 **yellow**.

Color sails with answers = 50 with **stripes**.

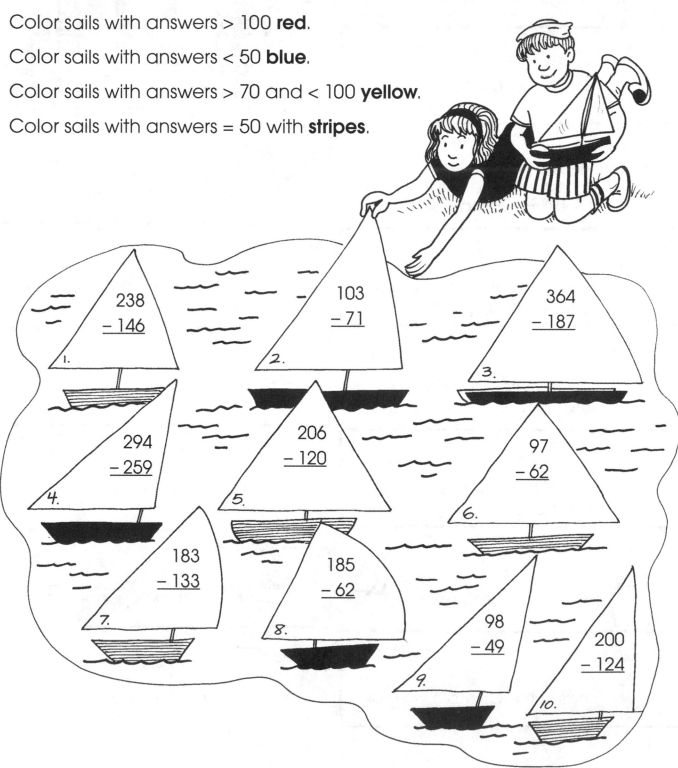

1. $238 - 146$	2. $103 - 71$	3. $364 - 187$
4. $294 - 259$	5. $206 - 120$	6. $97 - 62$
7. $183 - 133$	8. $185 - 62$	9. $98 - 49$
		10. $200 - 124$

Name _____

Snowball Subtraction

Every time a snowball is thrown, it has to be subtracted from the stack of snowballs!

1. Sal has thrown 117 of her snowballs. She started with 590. How many does she have left?

   _____

2. Skip made 999 snowballs. He has 45 left. How many did he throw?

   _____

Solve the rest of the snowball subtraction problems.

3.　　271 snowballs
　　　– 44 thrown
　　　　　left

4.　　116 snowballs
　　　–10 left
　　　　thrown

5.　　912 snowballs
　　　– 224 left
　　　　thrown

6.　　138 snowballs
　　　– 109 thrown
　　　　　left

7.　　833 snowballs
　　　– 461 left
　　　　thrown

8.　　600 snowballs
　　　–567 thrown
　　　　left

9.　　952 snowballs
　　　– 64 left
　　　　thrown

10.　　505 snowballs
　　　– 333 thrown
　　　　left

Name _____

+ and – within 1000

Homework at the Gym

GYMNASTIC PRACTICE

We did our homework at the gym. Did we do a good job?

Check all their answers.
Circle any wrong answers. Fix them.
Who has the most right answers?

_____

Terry

A. 17
+97
117

B. 56
−23
33

C. 106
+14
110

D. 234
−214
20

Kerry

E. 372
+419
781

F. 64
+56
120

G. 487
+74
561

H. 312
+486
798

Mary

I. 42
89
+15
146

J. 5
3
+8
17

K. 34
44
+54
132

L. 642
−161
803

Barry

M. 112
−56
56

N. 328
+67
387

O. 550
−275
285

P. 300
−179
121

Name _____

Muggy Workouts

The swamp can be a hot and muggy place, especially when you are exercising.

Read about the swamp critters and their workouts. Circle the answer to each problem.

1. Fifi Frog jumped rope so many times! Her number was 90 times 8. Circle the number of times she jumped.

    98   980   720

2. Slicky Snake did 50 pushups on Monday. Sammy Snake did 5 times that many. What was the number of Sammy's pushups?

    500   250   25

3. Pokey Porcupine did a whole lot of jumping jacks. The number he did was 60 times 7. How many jumping jacks did Pokey jump?

    420   67   560

4. Catfish workouts include flying leaps in the air. Big Daddy did 20. Big Mama did twice that many. Big Sissy did twice as many as Mama. How many leaps did Sissy do?

    60   100   80

5. Cranky Crocodile swam 80 laps in the swamp. Charlie swam 4 times that many. How many laps did Charlie swim?

    84   840   320

6. Six friends jogged for 8 miles each. How many miles, total, did they jog?

    80   86   680
    48   84   480

7. Molly Muskrat did tail lifts for 6 hours. She did 12,000. How many times did she lift her tail each hour?

    18   1000   100
    2000   200   180

8. Darla Dragonfly stretched for 40 minutes. She did 9 stretches a minute. How many stretches did she do in all?

    409   49   36
    400   360   490

Name

Multiply with multiples of 10

Noises in the Woods

The campers keep hearing spooky sounds. What things might be hiding in the woods? You'll find out when you solve the problems.

Follow the Color Code to color the puzzle pieces. (Some things might be upside down!)

60 x 3 =

30 x 5 =

90 x 4 =

60 x 5 =

5 x 90 =

2 x 90 =

600 x 8 =

800 x 6 =

$\begin{array}{r} 40 \\ \times 9 \\ \hline \end{array}$

$\begin{array}{r} 60 \\ \times 6 \\ \hline \end{array}$

$\begin{array}{r} 80 \\ \times 9 \\ \hline \end{array}$

$\begin{array}{r} 700 \\ \times 70 \\ \hline \end{array}$

$\begin{array}{r} 600 \\ \times 8 \\ \hline \end{array}$

$\begin{array}{r} 400 \\ \times 5 \\ \hline \end{array}$

1000 x 2 =

8 x 800 =

$\begin{array}{r} 50 \\ \times 4 \\ \hline \end{array}$

$\begin{array}{r} 20 \\ \times 3 \\ \hline \end{array}$

6 x 50 =

$\begin{array}{r} 90 \\ \times 8 \\ \hline \end{array}$

$\begin{array}{r} 100 \\ \times 3 \\ \hline \end{array}$

Name

NUMBER
AND
OPERATIONS— FRACTIONS

Grade 3

Dance Till You Drop

At the Swampville Line Dancing Contest, the last one left dancing is the winner. These dancers are still going strong!

There are 6 dancers. 1 of them is singing. So, $\frac{1}{6}$ of the dancers are singing. There are 12 feet. On 2 of the feet there are work boots. So, $\frac{2}{12}$ of the feet have on work boots.

Write a fraction to answer each question.

1. What fraction of the dancers are wearing skirts? _____

2. What fraction of the dancers are wearing hats? _____

3. What fraction of the dancers have on vests? _____

4. What fraction of the dancers are prickly? _____

5. What fraction of the dancers have a hair flower? _____

6. What fraction of the feet are wearing cowboy boots? _____

7. What fraction of the feet are bare feet? _____

8. What fraction of the feet are bear feet? _____

9. What fraction of the bandannas are black? _____

10. What fraction of the vests have fringe? _____

11. What fraction of the girls have hair bows? _____

12. What fraction of the skirts have flowers? _____

13. What fraction of the skirts have fringe? _____

14. What fraction of the hats are white? _____

Name

Swimmers Line-up

The top number is the **numerator**. It answers the question.

The bottom number is the **denominator**. It tells how many in all.

The swim team is ready for the big race. Let's take a look at all their equipment!

$\frac{6}{6}$ of the swimmers are ready to go!

Write a fraction to answer each question.

_____ 1. How many swimmers have goggles?

_____ 2. How many feet have on fins?

_____ 3. How many swimmers are wearing suits with stripes?

_____ 4. How many swimmers are still wet?

_____ 5. How many swimmers are wearing bathing caps?

_____ 6. How many feet have aqua socks?

_____ 7. How many swimmers have a float?

_____ 8. How many suits have NO dots?

_____ 9. How many noses have a nose plug?

_____ 10. How many suits are black?

Name

Fractional Parts

Pizza Party

A **mixed numeral** is a number that shows a whole number and a fraction.

The football players were really hungry after their games.
They all ate a lot of pizza. Who ate the most?
Write mixed numerals to show how much each player ate.

Rocky ate _____   Ernest ate _____   Bruiser ate _____

Jess ate _____   Kujo ate _____   Bud ate _____

Who ate the most? _____   Who left the most? _____

Name _____

Fractional Parts

Frisbee™ Fractions

Which Frisbee™ is which?
Write the letter to tell which Frisbee™
matches each description.

___ 1. $\frac{6}{6}$ dotted

___ 2. $\frac{2}{3}$ striped

___ 3. $\frac{1}{2}$ stars

___ 4. $\frac{1}{4}$ white

___ 5. $\frac{9}{12}$ white

___ 6. $\frac{3}{8}$ dotted

___ 7. $\frac{4}{6}$ white

___ 8. $\frac{1}{12}$ black

___ 9. $\frac{2}{7}$ stars

___ 10. $\frac{1}{1}$ flowered

___ 11. $\frac{1}{3}$ stars

___ 12. $\frac{3}{3}$ black

___ 13. $\frac{1}{2}$ white

___ 14. $\frac{1}{12}$ stars

___ 15. $\frac{1}{7}$ stripes

___ 16. $\frac{1}{8}$ checkered

Name _____

Fractional Parts

Dinner at Dino's Diner

All the teams eat lunch at Dino's Diner.

Read each fraction to see how much pizza a team has eaten.

For problems 1 to 5, color the pizzas to show what they ate.

1. The Frog Legs ate $2\frac{2}{3}$ pizzas.

2. The Possum Pistols ate $3\frac{1}{6}$ pizzas.

3. The Alligator Alleycats ate $3\frac{5}{6}$ pizzas.

4. The Ladybugs ate $1\frac{7}{8}$ pizzas.

6. The Turtle Terrors left _____?

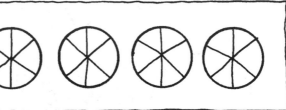

5. The Pelican Pitchers ate $2\frac{2}{5}$ pizzas.

7. The Slippery Snakes left _____.

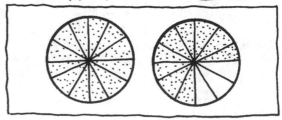

The Racing Skunks

The skunk sisters are off to the Hokee Penokee Skunk races. They will watch some friends race on a long, straight track.

Follow the directions for each problem.

1. Write the missing fraction to show how much of the track Sid has covered so far.

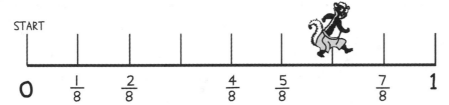

2. Write the missing fraction to show how much of the track Sasha has covered so far.

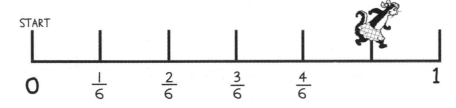

3. Write the fractions to finish numbering the race track. Then draw a skunk who has finished 3/5 of the track.

4. Write the fractions to finish numbering the race track. Then draw three racing skunks at 3/10, 6/10, and 9/10.

Name

Fractions on Number Line

Log-Throwing Champions

Log throwing is not an easy sport! Bosco is one of the athletes to compete today. Each athlete has his or her name on the log.

Write fractions to finish each number line on the log-throwing field.

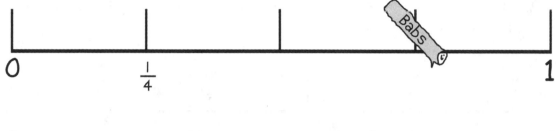

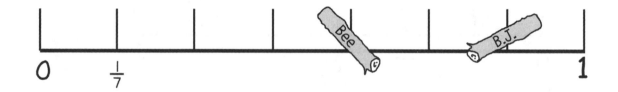

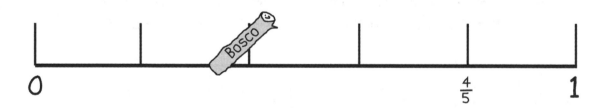

Write a name to answer each question.

1. Whose log has landed at $\frac{2}{5}$ the length of the field? _____

2. Whose log has landed at $\frac{4}{7}$ the length of the field? _____

3. Whose log has landed at $\frac{2}{3}$ the length of the field? _____

4. Whose log has landed at $\frac{3}{4}$ the length of the field? _____

Name

Where's the Golf Ball?

When Chester plays golf, the ball often ends up in the swamp!

Finally, he gets the ball back on the golf course. He hits some nice, straight shots.

The number line shows how far he has hit the ball.

1. Chester hits the ball $\frac{1}{4}$ of the way to the hole. Draw a red ball to show this distance.

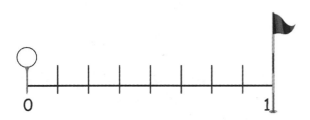

3. He hits the next ball $\frac{1}{6}$ of the way to the hole. Draw a green ball to show this distance.

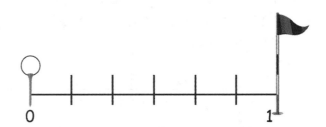

2. Chester hits the next ball $\frac{1}{8}$ of the way to the hole. Draw a blue ball to show this distance.

4. He hits the next ball $\frac{1}{2}$ of the way to the hole. Draw an orange ball to show this distance.

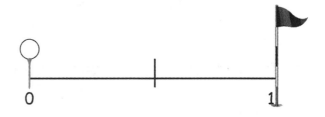

Name

Fractions on Number Line

The Great Bug Race

Two fractions are equivalent when they show the same amount.

Two equivalent fractions will be at the same spot on a number line.

Look at the pair of number lines to see where each bug is.

Write fractions in the blanks to finish each sentence.

1. These two bugs have covered the same distance on a number line.

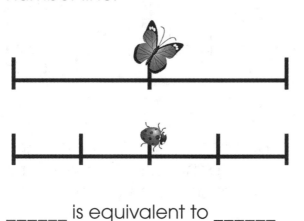

   _____ is equivalent to _____

2. These two bugs have covered the same distance on a number line.

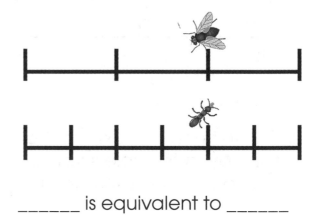

   _____ is equivalent to _____

3. These two bugs have covered the same distance on a number line.

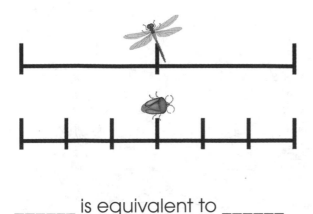

   _____ is equivalent to _____

4. These two bugs have covered the same distance on a number line.

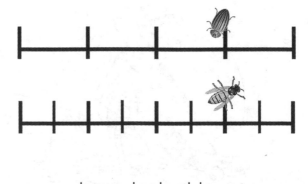

   _____ is equivalent to _____

Name _____

Equivalent Fractions

68

Bayou Bouncers

The baby alligators are bouncing on the boggy trampoline in the bayou. Each one uses a fraction of the trampoline space. Read what they say.

Look at the mini trampoline examples.

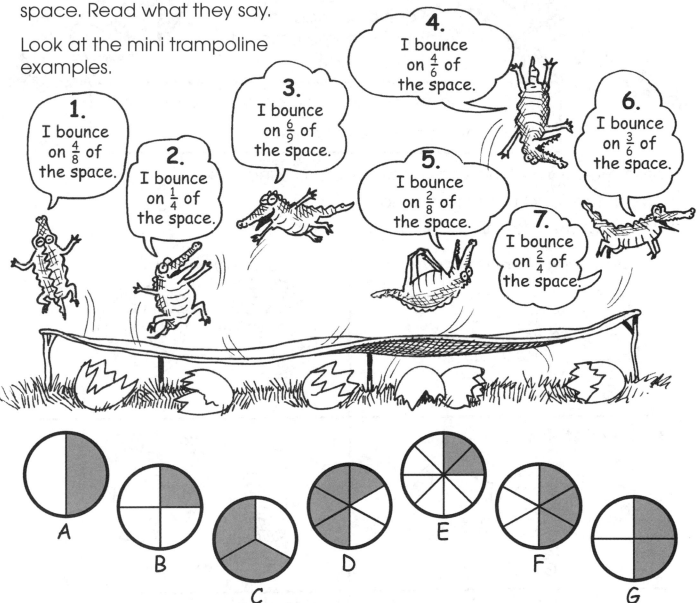

Write an alligator's letter to answer each question.

1. Which alligator jumps on the same size space as E? _____

2. Which alligators jump on the same size space as C? _____

3. Which alligators jump on the same size space as A? _____

Name _____

Copyright © Incentive Publications
Common Core Reinforcement Activities — 3rd Grade Math

Equivalent Fractions

Lunch on the Mountaintop

Equivalent fractions name the same amount of something.

$\frac{1}{2}$ of a sandwich is the same amount as $\frac{2}{4}$ of it.

So we say that $\frac{1}{2}$ is **equivalent** to $\frac{2}{4}$. Write $\frac{1}{2} = \frac{2}{4}$.

These mountain climbers have stopped for lunch.
Look at the food they are eating.
Write fractions that are equivalent to each other.

1. Tuna and Sprout Sandwich

$$\frac{1}{2} = \frac{}{4}$$

2. Whole wheat pizza

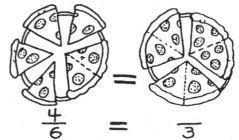

$$\frac{4}{6} = \frac{}{3}$$

3. Low fat Swiss cheese

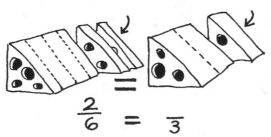

$$\frac{2}{6} = \frac{}{3}$$

4. Mega "C" Soda

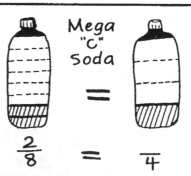

$$\frac{2}{8} = \frac{}{4}$$

5. Chocolate Energy Squares

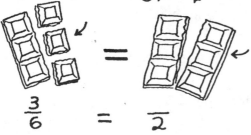

$$\frac{3}{6} = \frac{}{2}$$

6. Health Nut Loaf

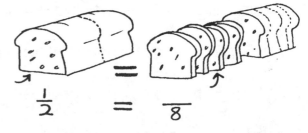

$$\frac{1}{2} = \frac{}{8}$$

Name _____

River-Bottom Surprises

Ollie and Ara Otter are so curious! They have spotted a bunch of fractions on the bottom of the river.

Write one or two of the fractions to answer each question.

1. Ollie found $\frac{2}{6}$. What other fraction is the same size? _____

2. Ara found $\frac{1}{2}$. What other fractions are the same size? _____

3. Ollie found $\frac{2}{3}$. What other fraction is the same size? _____

4. Ara found $\frac{6}{8}$. What other fraction is the same size? _____

5. Ollie found $\frac{2}{5}$. What other fraction is the same size? _____

6. Ara found $\frac{1}{5}$. What other fraction is the same size? _____

For 7 and 8, color the second shape to show a fraction the same size as the fraction colored in the first shape. Write the fractions.

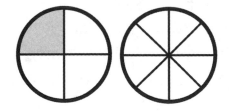

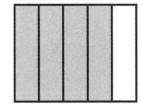

7. _____ is equivalent to _____

8. _____ is equivalent to _____

$\frac{6}{9}$ $\frac{2}{3}$ $\frac{2}{4}$ $\frac{2}{5}$

$\frac{4}{10}$ $\frac{1}{5}$ $\frac{2}{10}$

$\frac{3}{4}$ $\frac{4}{8}$ $\frac{1}{2}$

$\frac{2}{6}$ $\frac{1}{3}$

$\frac{1}{2}$ $\frac{6}{8}$

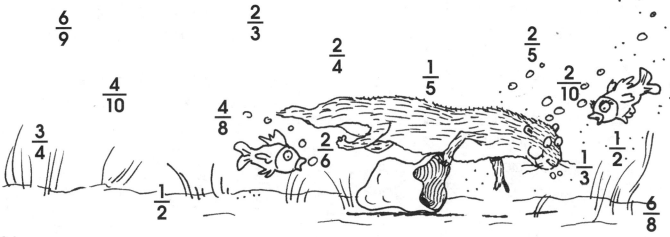

Name _____

Equivalent Fractions

The Swamp's Strongest Lifters

It's time for the weightlifting contest in Hokee Penokee Swamp. The swamp critters lift the biggest rocks they can find.

Even the smallest creatures want to be in the contest. Tiny Lucy Ladybug can lift $\frac{7}{10}$ of a kilogram!

Circle the correct answer for each problem.

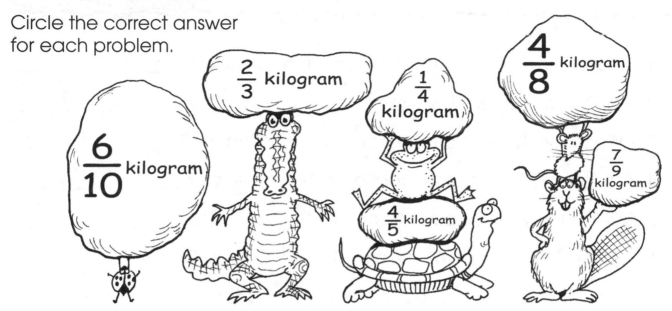

1. Which fraction is equivalent to the weight of frog's rock?
   - a. $\frac{3}{6}$ kilogram
   - c. $\frac{2}{8}$ kilogram
   - b. $\frac{1}{2}$ kilogram
   - d. $\frac{2}{5}$ kilogram

2. Which animals are holding the same amount of weight?
   - a. ladybug and turtle
   - b. alligator and frog
   - c. mouse and beaver
   - d. no two animals

3. Which fraction is equivalent to the weight of beaver's rock?
   - a. $\frac{14}{18}$ kilogram
   - c. $\frac{2}{3}$ kilogram
   - b. $\frac{1}{2}$ kilogram
   - d. $\frac{3}{4}$ kilogram

4. Which animal's rock is equivalent to $\frac{8}{16}$ kilogram?
   - a. frog
   - c. turtle
   - b. mouse
   - d. alligator

5. Which fraction is equivalent to the weight of ladybug's rock?
   - a. $\frac{3}{4}$ kilogram
   - c. $\frac{3}{5}$ kilogram
   - b. $\frac{1}{2}$ kilogram
   - d. $\frac{2}{3}$ kilogram

6. Which animal's rock is equivalent to $\frac{8}{10}$ kilogram?
   - a. ladybug
   - b. beaver
   - c. turtle
   - d. alligator

Name

Equivalent Fractions

72

Common Core Reinforcement Activities — 3rd Grade Math

Obstacles in the Swamp

Arthur loves to jet ski around the swamp.

He must use all his skill, because the swamp is full of obstacles.

Look at the obstacles in the swamp. Read the fractional numbers on them.

Look in the picture. Find the fractional number that matches each set of words below. Write the number next to the words.

Color the part of the picture after you have used the number.

1. ten and four fifths _____

2. five and three fourths _____

3. three and one fourth _____

4. number equivalent to $\frac{1}{2}$ _____

5. numbers equivalent to 1 _____

_____

6. five and six tenths _____

7. ten halves _____

8. two and two fourths_____

9. two and three halves_____

10. number equivalent to $\frac{23}{4}$ _____

11. number equivalent to $\frac{4}{8}$ _____

Name

Copyright © Incentive Publications
Common Core Reinforcement Activities — 3rd Grade Math

Whole Number Fractions

Daring Dives

The judges at the diving contest were dazzled by Flossie! She performed her famous jackknife dive very well.

The judges each gave Flossie a score of $\frac{90}{10}$ points. This score means the same as the whole number 9.

The fraction $\frac{90}{10}$ is **equivalent to** 9. ($\approx$ means equivalent.)

Write the whole number that is equivalent to these fractions.

1. $\frac{12}{12} \approx$ _____

2. $\frac{8}{8} \approx$ _____

3. $\frac{100}{100} \approx$ _____

4. $\frac{40}{10} \approx$ _____

5. $\frac{70}{10} \approx$ _____

6. $\frac{100}{10} \approx$ _____

7. $\frac{30}{3} \approx$ _____

8. $\frac{20}{20} \approx$ _____

9. $\frac{60}{10} \approx$ _____

10. $\frac{9}{9} \approx$ _____

11. $\frac{6}{6} \approx$ _____

12. $\frac{15}{15} \approx$ _____

Name _____

Swamp Flip-Flop

Finn and Flossy Frog are enjoying a good game of blanket toss. They are hopping, flipping, and flopping all over the place.

Keep track of all the places they land. Write the answer. If there is a color word, use that color to fill the answer space on the blanket.

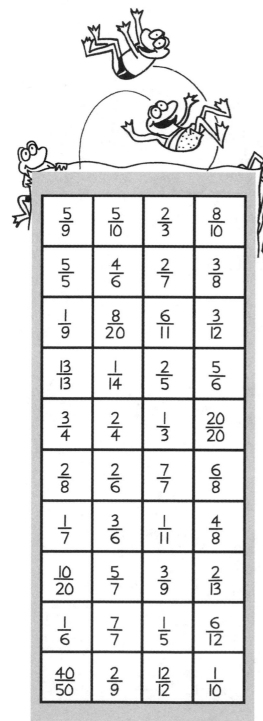

1. Frannie does $\frac{4}{5}$ of a turn.
   Which fractions are $\approx \frac{4}{5}$?
   Color the squares BLUE.

2. Finn twists $\frac{1}{4}$ turn.
   Which fractions are $\approx \frac{1}{4}$?
   Color the squares RED.

3. Frannie does one full flip.
   Which fractions are ≈ 1?
   Color the squares PURPLE.

4. Finn does $\frac{4}{14}$ of a flip.
   Which fraction is $\approx \frac{4}{14}$?
   Color the square GREEN.

5. Frannie twists $\frac{4}{10}$ of a turn.
   Which fraction is $\approx \frac{4}{10}$?
   Color the square YELLOW.

6. Finn jumps $\frac{1}{3}$ of the way to
   the ceiling! What fraction is $\approx \frac{1}{3}$?
   Color the square BROWN.

7. Frannie does a half flip.
   Which fractions are $\approx \frac{1}{2}$?
   Color the squares PINK.

8. Is there a fraction on the blanket
   that is larger than $\frac{12}{12}$?

   Circle yes or no.   yes   no

Name _____

Copyright © Incentive Publications
Common Core Reinforcement Activities — 3rd Grade Math

Whole Number Fractions, Equivalent Fractions

The Great Shell Race

The Bogtown Racers team was ahead for $\frac{1}{4}$ of the race.

Now, the Swampville Hardshells are in the lead. They have been ahead for $\frac{2}{4}$ of the race. Who has been in the lead the longest?

The answer is—the Hardshells, because $\frac{2}{4}$ is more than $\frac{1}{4}$.

Circle the answer to each question about comparing fractions.

1. Which fraction is greater? $\qquad$ $\frac{6}{8}$ $\qquad$ $\frac{4}{8}$

2. Which fraction is the largest? $\quad$ $\frac{1}{4}$ $\quad$ $\frac{4}{4}$ $\quad$ $\frac{3}{4}$ $\quad$ $\frac{6}{4}$ $\quad$ $\frac{2}{4}$

3. Which is less than $1\frac{3}{4}$? $\qquad$ $3\frac{3}{4}$ $\quad$ $1\frac{1}{4}$ $\quad$ $2\frac{1}{4}$ $\quad$ $2\frac{3}{4}$

4. Which shows an amount greater than $\frac{12}{3}$? $\quad$ $\frac{11}{3}$ $\quad$ $\frac{9}{3}$ $\quad$ $\frac{6}{4}$ $\quad$ $\frac{10}{3}$ $\quad$ $\frac{15}{3}$

Write <, >, or = in each space.

5. $\frac{7}{2}$ ☐ $\frac{2}{2}$ 9. $\frac{16}{5}$ ☐ $\frac{15}{5}$

6. $\frac{2}{10}$ ☐ $\frac{4}{20}$ 10. $100\frac{1}{2}$ ☐ $100\frac{1}{4}$

7. $\frac{2}{5}$ ☐ $\frac{4}{5}$ 11. $\frac{1}{2}$ ☐ $\frac{5}{10}$

8. $\frac{1}{2}$ ☐ $\frac{2}{2}$ 12. $\frac{10}{10}$ ☐ $\frac{8}{8}$

Name

Picnic Problems

Oh, oh! Some things have gone wrong at the Hokee Penokee Picnic.

Read about the problems. Then find the answers.

A. $\frac{4}{5}$ of the boiled bumblebee nests were spoiled by the rain. Is this amount more than all of the nests?

_____

B. $\frac{2}{3}$ pounds of the barbecue bark chips washed away into the swamp. Is this more or less than $\frac{1}{3}$ pound?

_____

C. Tootsie Turtle and Freddy Frog ate too much. Freddy ate $42\frac{4}{5}$ swamp moss pancakes. Tootsie ate $42\frac{2}{5}$ swamp moss pancakes. Who ate more?

_____

D. $\frac{5}{9}$ of the frozen chocolate slush mud servings melted. Another $\frac{2}{9}$ got sat on by Grandma Crocodile. How much was ruined in all?

_____

E. The baby frogs found the candied bugs before the feast. Baby Fran ate $6\frac{1}{2}$. Baby Frankie ate $2\frac{1}{2}$ bugs. All together, did they eat more than 10 bugs?

_____

F. Cook ordered $222\frac{3}{4}$ pounds of swamp cookies for the feast. Only 200 pounds came. How many pounds of cookies were missing?

_____

G. Only $\frac{3}{7}$ of the stuffed moss ball appetizers were ready on time. Is this amount more or less than $\frac{1}{7}$?

_____

H. The Floppy Mud Puppy Band arrived $3\frac{1}{4}$ hours late because their boat got tangled in tree roots. The singers arrived $3\frac{3}{4}$ hours late. Who arrived later, the band or the singers?

_____

Name

Compare Fractions

Some Fishy Problems

Pokey Porcupine and Finn Frog are fishing for "problems" today.
Who will catch the most?

Write the symbol that is missing from each number sentence. (<, >, or =)

Finn is fishing for "greater than" problems.
How many of these are in the water? ___

Pokey is fishing for "less than" problems.
How many of these are in the water? ___

A. $\dfrac{6}{8}$ ☐ $\dfrac{3}{8}$

B. $\dfrac{12}{12}$ ☐ $\dfrac{5}{5}$

C. $\dfrac{8}{3}$ ☐ $\dfrac{4}{3}$

D. $10\dfrac{1}{2}$ ☐ $11\dfrac{1}{2}$

E. $\dfrac{7}{7}$ ☐ 1

F. $\dfrac{20}{40}$ ☐ $\dfrac{2}{4}$

G. $\dfrac{9}{10}$ ☐ $\dfrac{3}{10}$

H. 1 ☐ $\dfrac{9}{8}$

I. $\dfrac{6}{5}$ ☐ $\dfrac{5}{5}$

J. $\dfrac{4}{10}$ ☐ $\dfrac{2}{5}$

K. $\dfrac{5}{2}$ ☐ $\dfrac{1}{2}$

L. $\dfrac{3}{4}$ ☐ $\dfrac{6}{8}$

M. $\dfrac{11}{11}$ ☐ $\dfrac{10}{10}$

Name _____

MEASUREMENT
AND
DATA

Grade 3

Sara's Sports Schedule

Sara is busy with many sports. She has to keep a schedule. Each clock tells what time it is when Sara arrives at one of the events.

For each problem, circle **yes** if she is on time or a bit early. Circle **no** if she is late or much too early.

Soccer Practice	Monday 6:30 P.M.	Chess Club	Tuesday 5:15 P.M.
Ski Meet	Saturday 11:00 A.M.	Bowling Team	Thursday 1:45 P.M.
Dance Lessons	Tuesday 2:45 P.M.	Batting Cage	Thursday 4:20 P.M.
Tennis Match	Friday 4:10 P.M.	Ice Skating Practice	Thursday 4:20 P.M.

Is she on time?

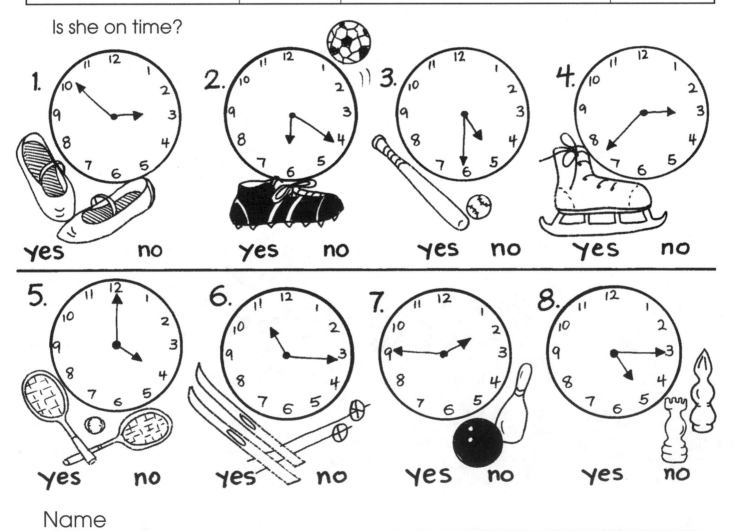

1. yes   no

2. yes   no

3. yes   no

4. yes   no

5. yes   no

6. yes   no

7. yes   no

8. yes   no

Name

A Very Silly Field Day

Some very silly events are taking place at the Laugh-a-Lot School Field Day.

Help the timekeeper with some time problems.

The first clock shows when an event starts.
The words tell how long each event takes.

Show what time the event ends.

Draw hands on the clocks, or write in the time.

1. Running Egg Dodge
took
15 min.
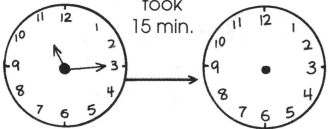

2. Ear Wiggling Marathon
took
½ hour
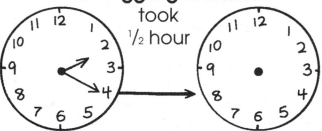

3. Popsicle Relay
took
20 min.
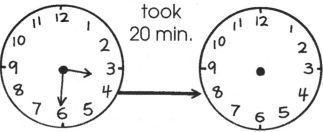

4. Lunch
took
1 hour
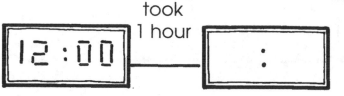

5. Headstand in Water
took
40 min.

6. Baby Buggy Races
took
30 min.
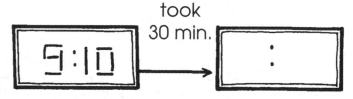

7. Banana Peel Slide
took
45 min.
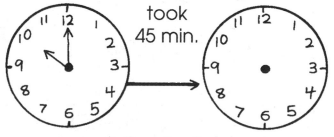

8. Toaster Toss
took
20 min.
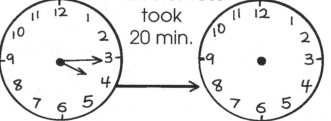

Name

Telling Time, Time Problems

Field Day Math

Field Day is an exciting day for all the kids at Walker School.

Every student needs to know the time of the events.

The schedule is posted on the fence.

Use the Field Day Schedule to solve the problems on the next page (page 83).

I'm here for the Hop, Skip, and Jump Contest

FROG-EE

FIELD DAY — WALKER SCHOOL

TIME	FIELD 1	FIELD 2
9:00 A.M.	Sign-ups	Sign-ups
9:30 A.M.	3-Legged Race	Water Balloon Toss
9:45 A.M.	100-Yard Potato Sack Hop	Softball Throw
10:00 A.M.	4-Person Relay Races	Bubble Gum-Blowing Contest
11:00 A.M.	↓	Frisbee™ Tournament
11:30 A.M.	Hop, Skip, & Jump	↓
12:00 P.M.	Lunch	Lunch
1:00 P.M.	Teacher-Kid Softball Game	Bike Rodeo
3:15 P.M.	Squirt Gun Target Shoot	Watermelon-Eating Contest
4:00 P.M.	Award Ceremony (Ribbons) and Barbecue	

Use with page 83.

Name

Field Day Math, continued

Use the schedule on page 82 to help answer the questions.

1. Gracie gets to the field at 9:20 A.M.
   Does she have time to sign up for an event?

   _____

2. Trudy has a ballet class at 5:00 P.M. Can she
   compete in the watermelon-eating contest?

   _____

3. Name 2 events that take only 15 minutes.

   _____

   and

   _____

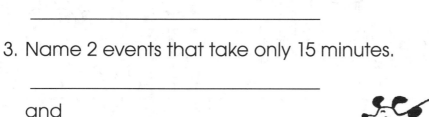

4. Name an event that takes 1 hour.

   _____

5. Steve looks at his watch. It is 11:30 A.M.
   How many minutes are there until lunch?

   _____

6. What time will the Frisbee™ tournament end?

   _____

7. How much time is allowed for the softball game? _____

8. How much time does the schedule allow for relay races? _____

9. Al's friend Margie wants him to run the 3-legged race with her.
   He gets to Field 1 at 9:40 A.M. Is he early, late, or on time?

   _____

10. Erik wins a blue ribbon in the bike rodeo.
    What time will he go to get his award? _____

Use with page 82.

Name

Telling Time, Time Problems

Could You Swim in a Cup?

Could the Ladybug Swim Team swim in a cup of water? Probably not, unless they are really bugs!

A cup does not hold much water.

A cup holds 16 tablespoons of water.

A pint holds 2 cups.

A quart holds 4 cups (or 2 pints).

A gallon holds 4 quarts (or 8 pints or 16 cups).

cup   pint   quart   gallon

Which unit would you use to measure each of these amounts? Circle the best unit.

1. water in a pool
   cups   gallons

2. water in a bathtub
   quarts   gallons

3. water in a water bed
   pints   gallons

4. water in a river
   quarts   gallons

5. sports drink in a glass
   cups   gallons

THIRST-ADE

6. milk for a team of 20 players
   cups   gallons

MILK

Name

Taking the Plunge

These critters always head for water on hot days.

Try to decide how much water is in each container before they take the plunge into the water!

Circle the measurement that is the best estimate for the amount of water in each container.

A liter is about the size of a quart. Write L to mean liter.

1. $\frac{1}{4}$ L   10 L

2. 100 L   1 L

3. 2 L   20 L

4. 2 L   300 L

5. 7 L   7000 L

6. 10 L   10,000 L

7. 3 L   300 L

8. 5 L   5000 L

Color the pictures.

Name

Measure Liquid Volume

Weighty Questions

How would you measure a horse?

If you wanted to measure its weight, which unit of weight would you use?

> oz — ounce
> lb — pound (1 lb = 16 ounces)
> t — ton (1 t = 2000 pounds)

Write the best unit to weigh each of these things at a horse show.

1. Hannah's horse _____

2. Hannah _____

3. Hannah's blue ribbon _____

4. Hannah's boots _____

5. Hannah's gloves _____

6. the horse's blanket _____

7. an apple for the horse _____

8. the truck that
   carries 10 horses _____

9. Hannah's shirt_____

10. the horse's shoes _____

11. Hannah weighs 73 pounds wearing all her riding clothes. Without the boots, she weighs 69 pounds. How much do her boots weigh?

_____

12. A big horse trailer weighs two tons. Ramon's horse weighs 2950 pounds less. How much does his horse weigh?

_____

Name

More Weighty Questions

A beach ball is too light for bowling.

A bowling ball wouldn't float very well in the ocean.

Their weights are very different.

What would you use to measure their weights?

Write **g** or **kg** as the best unit for measuring each of the things below.

table tennis ball

A table tennis ball weighs about a gram (g).

shoes

A pair of shoes weighs about a kilogram (kg).

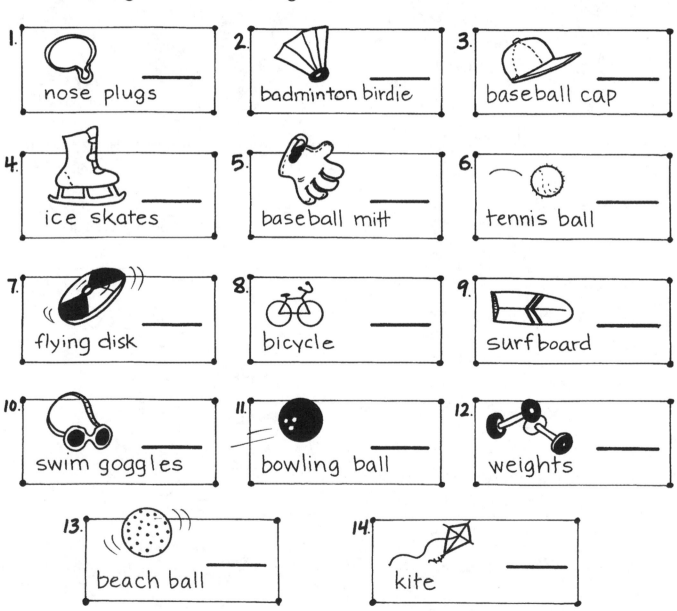

1. nose plugs _____

2. badminton birdie _____

3. baseball cap _____

4. ice skates _____

5. baseball mitt _____

6. tennis ball _____

7. flying disk _____

8. bicycle _____

9. surfboard _____

10. swim goggles _____

11. bowling ball _____

12. weights _____

13. beach ball _____

14. kite _____

Name _____

Measure Mass

Bear Gymnastics

Belinda dreamed that all of her teddy bears went to a gymnastics meet.

Lots of measuring went on at the meet.

Solve the measurement problems for the bears.

1. Elizabear is balancing on the beam. She stayed on for 75 seconds without falling. Her second try was 1 minute less. How long did she stay on the second time?

_____

2. Fuzzy Bear weighs 45 pounds. Buzzy Bear weighs 73 pounds.

How much more does Buzzy weigh?

_____

3. When Maybear does her exercises, she likes the temperature to be 65°F. Today it is 80°F. How many degrees difference is this?

_____°

Is this cooler or warmer than she likes it to be?

_____

Use with page 89.

Name _____

Bear Gymnastics, continued

4. Shakesbear drank 4 quarts of bear juice before the competition. How many cups is that?

_____

5. When Tuffy stands on his head, his body is 5 feet, 7 inches from his toes to his hands. Scruffy's body is 4 feet, 3 inches from his toes to his hands. How much taller is Tuffy?

_____

6. Flip clears the vault by 7 inches. Flop clears it by 1 foot. How many inches higher does Flop jump?

_____

7. Beau Bear is doing tumbling on the mat. How many square units does the mat cover?

_____

Use with page 88.

Name _____

Measurement

Big Gulpers

This pogo jumping team gets very thirsty.

The graph shows how much they drink during a contest.
It also shows which drinks they choose at the sports drink stand.

Use a different color of crayon to color each row
of drinks. Then read the graph to answer the questions.

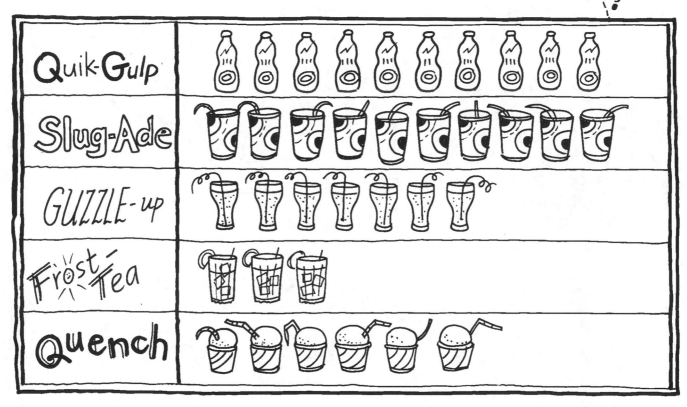

1. Which drink sold the least? _____

2. What is the total number of Slug-Ades and Frost-Teas drunk? _____

3. How many more Quik-Gulps than Guzzle-ups were sold? _____

4. How many more Guzzle-ups than Quenches were sold? _____

5. Which 2 drinks sold the same? _____ and _____

6. Pat drank 2 Frost Teas. How many were drunk by someone else? ____

7. Pam drank 4 Slug-Ades. How many more were sold? _____

8. Which was more popular, Quench or Slug-Ade? _____

Name
_____

Champion Jumpers

Read the chart to find out what happened at the
Frog Jumping Contest.
Then answer the questions.

Go!

Number Of Feet Jumped Each Day	Jumping Jake	Barney Bouncer	Harvey Hopper	Tilly Toad	Larry Leaper
Monday	4	8	2	4	6
Tuesday	6	8	4	6	2
Wednesday	8	4	2	6	8
Thursday	10	6	8	4	8
Friday	8	4	6	6	4

1. Who jumped farthest
   on Thursday? _____

2. What was Larry's worst day?
   _____

3. How many feet did Jake jump
   all week?
   _____

4. How far had Tilly jumped by the
   end of the day on Wednesday?
   _____

5. What was Harvey's best day?
   _____

6. Which days did Jake jump the
   same distance?
   _____

7. Which frogs jumped the same
   distance on Tuesday?
   _____

8. Who had the longest jump?
   _____

9. What were Barney's best days?
   _____

Name _____

Graphing, Data

Bumps and Lumps

aches and breaks

These skiers are in trouble! The graph tells about the injuries and sicknesses the ski team had this year. Read the graph. Answer the questions.

pains and sprains

1. How many skiers got sunburned? _____

2. Which injury did skiers get the most? _____

3. How many broken bones were there? _____

4. How many sprains were there? _____

5. Which injury happened 4 times? _____

6. Which injury happened 8 times? _____

7. How many more sprains than black eyes were there? _____

8. How many frostbites and sunburns were there all together? _____

9. Which injury happened the least? _____

10. How many more headaches than tummy aches were there? ____

Ski Team Aches & Pains									
sunburn	■	■	■	■	■	■				
broken bones	■									
sprains	■	■	■	■	■	■	■			
frostbite	■	■	■	■						
black eyes	■	■		■						
tummy aches	■	■	■	■						
headaches	■	■	■	■	■	■	■	■		
bruises	■	■	■	■	■	■	■	■	■	

Number of Injuries: 2   4   6   8   10   12   14   16   18   20

Name

Talented Feet

The Jetsville Junior Jumping Jacks are having fun at the jump rope jamboree.

Look at this table.

It tells how many times each jumper jumped without missing.

Judy	10
Jane	50
Jackie	80
Joey	90
Jenny	40
Jay	70
Jacob	100

Color in the bar graph to show the number of jumps for each jumper.

Use a different color marker for each bar.

Name _____

Graphing, Data

Sticks and Stuff

Melissa's stilts are taller than she is.

There are lots of sticks and poles and other long, narrow things in sports.

Measure the pictures of each of these pieces of long sports equipment.

Use a centimeter ruler, and write the measurement to the nearest centimeter.

1. Bat =_____cm

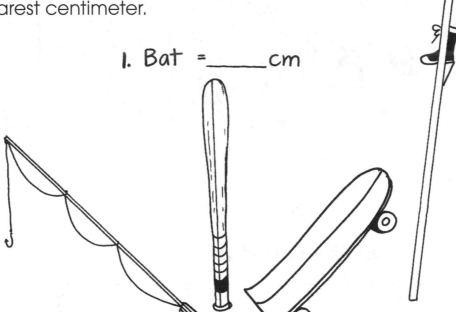

7. Stilts _____ cm

2. Fishing pole =____cm

6. Skateboard =_____cm

3. Golf club =____cm

4. Hockey stick =_____cm

5. Ski =_____cm

Name _____

Go Bugs!

The bugs are at it again! Every year they have a race to find out who can crawl or hop the farthest.

Measure the path for each bug from the end near the hand to the tip of the arrow. Use an inch ruler to measure each path. Write the number of inches each bug traveled. (Round to the nearest fourth of an inch.)

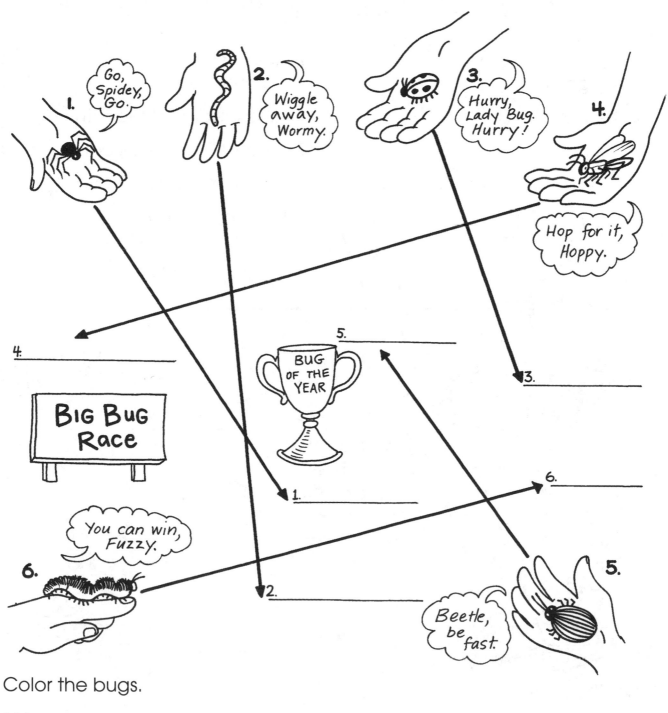

Color the bugs.

Name _____

Measure Length

Measurements at the Ball Field

Do you usually take a ruler to a baseball game? Probably not! But, how would you measure a hot dog or a baseball cap if you needed to?

Think about the units of measurement you would need. Tell what unit you would use to measure the real length of each of these.

1. around the diamond _____

2. how far the team traveled to get to the game _____

3. the bat's length _____

4. the pitcher's nose _____

5. your hot dog's length _____

6. the height of the grandstand _____

7. around the catcher's waist _____

8. a baseball mitt's length _____

9. around a baseball cap _____

10. around the scoreboard _____

11. from the pitcher's mound to home plate _____

12. length of the team's bus _____

Write inches, feet, or miles.

SCORE BOARD

Color the picture.

Name

Copyright © Incentive Publications
Common Core Reinforcement Activities — 3rd Grade Math

Can't Stop Measuring!

Harriet can't stop measuring things! She measures the distances she can jump. She also measures everyone's houses, pets, and even their noses and toes. She thinks it's fun.

Join her in the fun.
Use a ruler and a yardstick with inches and feet.
Measure as many of these things as you can find.

Label your measurements with inches or feet.
Round to the nearest inch.

Stop wagging!

HEY!

_____ 1. length of a nose

_____ 2. length of your foot

_____ 3. from your elbow to the tip of your thumb

_____ 4. width of your bedroom or classroom

_____ 5. height of a computer

_____ 6. length of your pillow

_____ 7. length of an eyebrow

_____ 8. length of your bathtub or shower

_____ 9. size of a sandwich

_____ 10. length of a book

_____ 11. length of your shoelace

_____ 12. height of a desk or table

_____ 13. height of your mom, dad, or teacher

_____ 14. height of your best friend

_____ 15. length of your friend's hand

_____ 16. length of someone's hair

Name

Copyright © Incentive Publications
Common Core Reinforcement Activities — 3rd Grade Math

Measure Length

Caterpillar Measurements

Tiny caterpillars can cover a lot of distance!
Look at Line Plot A to answer the questions.
Each X stands for one caterpillar who crawled that distance.

_____ 1. How many caterpillars crawled 5 yds?

_____ 2. How many crawled less than 2 yds?

_____ 3. How many crawled $3\frac{1}{2}$ yds?

_____ 4. How many crawled $2\frac{1}{2}$ yds?

Look at the list of caterpillars.
See how far they crawled.

Mark an X on Line Plot B above the distance for each caterpillar.

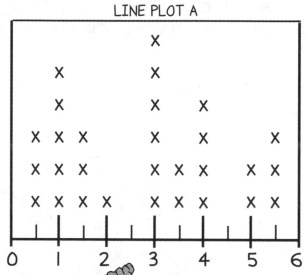

LINE PLOT A

LINE PLOT B

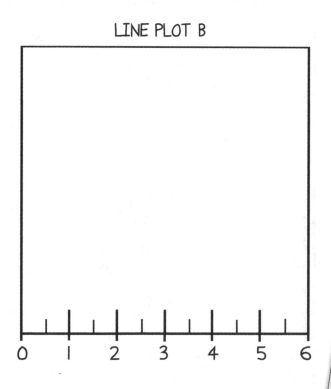

Fuzzy crawled 3½ yds.
Buzzy crawled 5 yds.
Slinky crawled 6 yds.
Nuzzle did not move from zero.
Lexi crawled 1½ yds.
Binky crawled as far as Slinky.
Stinky crawled 4½ yds.
Gooey crawled 3 yds.
Tooey crawled 3 yds.
Lucy crawled 2½ yds.
Mazie crawled 4½ yds.
Ozzie crawled 5 yds.

Name

Measure Length

Space on the Beach Blanket

Josie has left a lot of her beach stuff on her blanket.

About how much area does each thing cover?

Write the number that tells **about how many** squares each one covers.

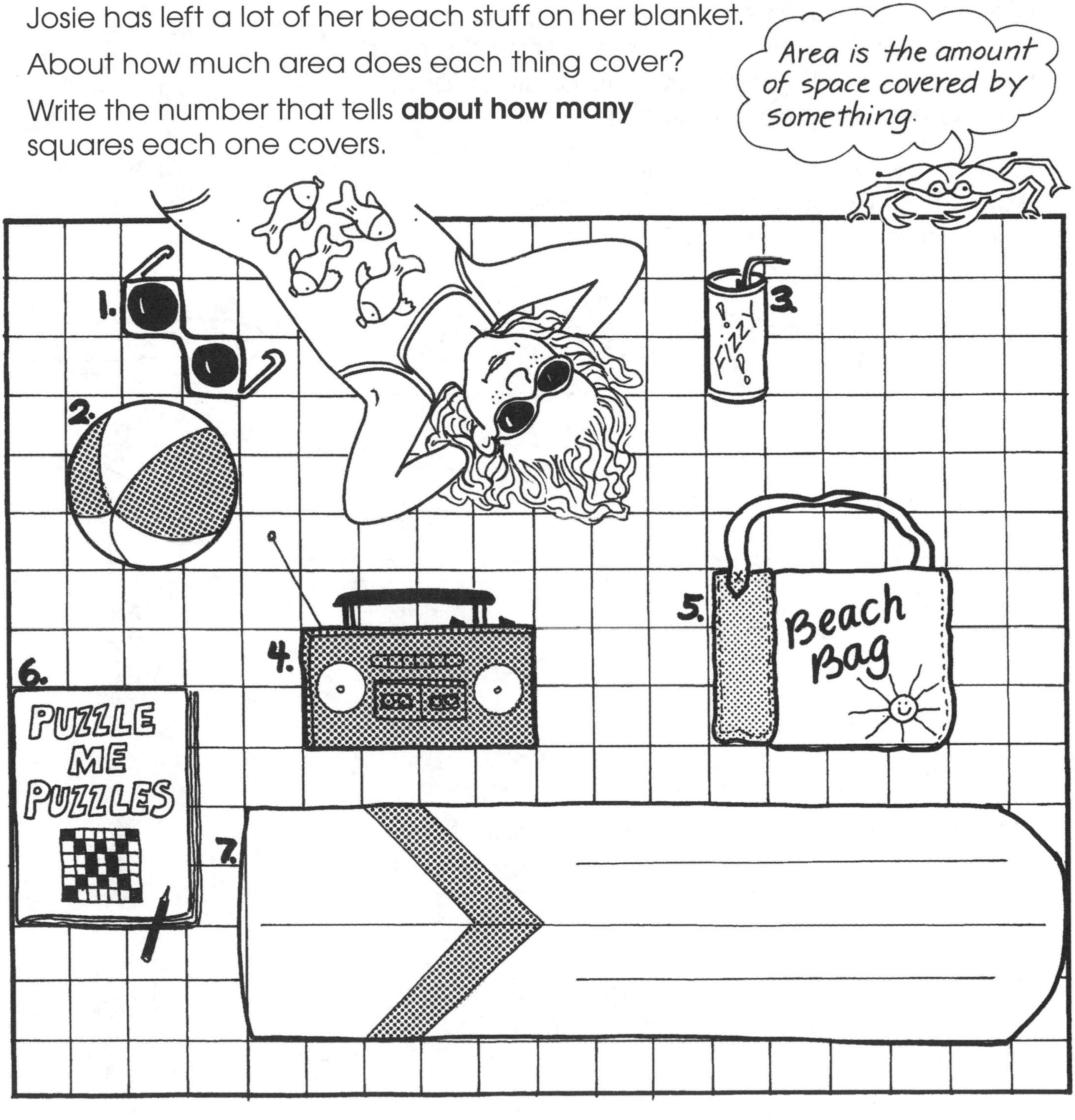

Area is the amount of space covered by something.

1. _____ square units   4. _____ square units   7. _____ square units

2. _____ square units   5. _____ square units   * Josie covers about _____ square units.

3. _____ square units   6. _____ square units

Name

Area Concepts

Visitors at a Picnic

Matt and Mandy are getting ready for a picnic with friends. See their picnic blanket on the next page (page 101). They have lots of great food, and some unexpected visitors!

Look at the things on their blanket.
About how many square units of area does each of these cover?

See their picnic blanket on the next page (page 101).

Remember: area is measured with square units.

1. soda cans (total)

_____

6. cell phone

_____

I smell a picnic ...

2. hot dog

_____

7. pie

_____

3. cake

_____

8. soccer ball

_____

4. tray with cookies

_____

9. tray with fish

_____

5. cupcakes (total)

_____

10. shoe

_____

Use with page 101.

Name _____

Visitors at a Picnic, continued

Use with page 100.

Name

Area Concepts

Cover Up!

Someone left a lot of sports equipment lying around the gym floor. Tell how much space each piece covers.

Area is the measure of how much space is covered by something. It is measured in square units.

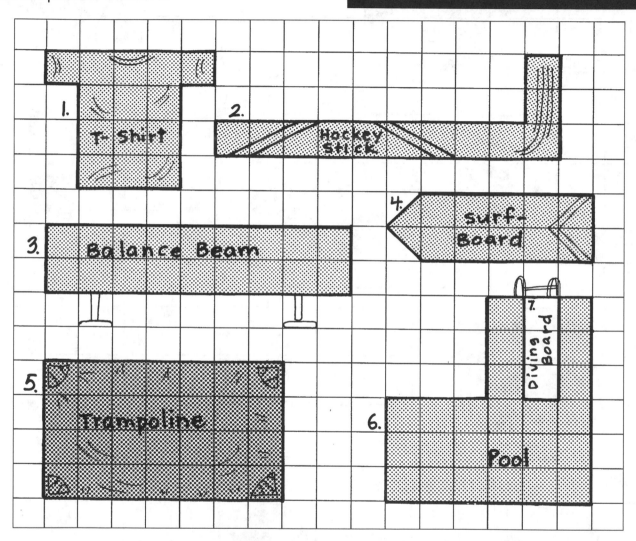

1. _____ square units

2. _____ square units

3. _____ square units

4. _____ square units

5. _____ square units

6. _____ square units

7. _____ square units

8. Which has the greatest area? _____

9. Which has the smallest area? _____

10. Which area is greater: the area of the T-shirt or the area of the hockey stick? _____

11. Do the beam and hockey stick have the same area? _____

Name

Sky-High Measurements

The sky is full of kites on school kite day.

Find the perimeter of each kite. Do not include tails, strings, or fringe.

Write the perimeter on the line inside each kite.

Decorate the kites to make them colorful.

Name

Perimeter

Terrific Banners

Shira and Shawn are making some great banners for their school soccer team, the Grizzlies.

Find the perimeter of each banner. Write this on the line with the matching number.

Decorate the banners to make them colorful.

1. P = _____

2. P = _____

3. P = _____

4. P = _____

5. P = _____

6. P = _____

7. P = _____

8. Which banner has the shortest perimeter?

_____

Banner 1: 11 in., 25 in., 22 in.

Banner 2: Ashland Grizzles! — 4 ft., 1 ft.

Banner 3: 47 in., 21 in. — Grrrrrrrrrrrrr

Banner 4: GO! — 24 in., 24 in.

Banner 5: Rah Rah Ra... — 3 ft., 1½ ft., 2 ft.

Banner 6: NO. 1 — 30 in., 30 in.

Banner 7: Sis boom bah — 13 in., 17 in.

A Strange Sale

Tara and Todd want some sports equipment. When they get to the store, they are surprised by what they find!

Look at the area covered by each object on the sale table.

Answer the questions.

1. What covers 8 square units? _____

2. What area can be shown by 4 x (3 + 1)? _____

3. What area can be shown by 2 x (2 + 5)? _____

4. What has more than 4 times the area of the SALE sign? _____

5. What area can be shown by 4 x (2 + 2)? _____

6. What area can be shown by 3 x (2 + 3)? _____

7. What is the difference between the largest and smallest areas?

_____

Name

Area Concepts

The Messy Room

Elijah's room is a mess! His stuff covers a lot of the area of his floor.

Find the areas to answer the questions.

If a figure has rectangles that overlap, find the area of parts that do not overlap and add those together.

1. **About how much** space is covered by both socks together?

   _____

2. What covers more area, the bed or the bookcase?

   _____

3. How much area is covered by the t-shirt?

   _____

4. How much area is covered by the rug with shoes and other stuff on it?

   _____

5. How much more area is covered by the pillow than one sock?

   _____

6. How much area is covered by the radio?

   _____

7. Is the area in the diagram that is uncovered greater than the area that is covered?

   _____

Name _____

Good Exercise

Gary's pet grasshopper, Garfus, is getting his exercise by hopping around the neighbors' gardens.

To find out how far he hopped, you will need to find the perimeter of each garden.

Write the number of feet Garfus hopped around each garden. You can add in your head or use a separate piece of paper.

Remember: Perimeter is the distance around the outside of a shape!

A. _____ ft   D. _____ ft   F. _____ ft

B. _____ ft   E. _____ ft

C. _____ ft

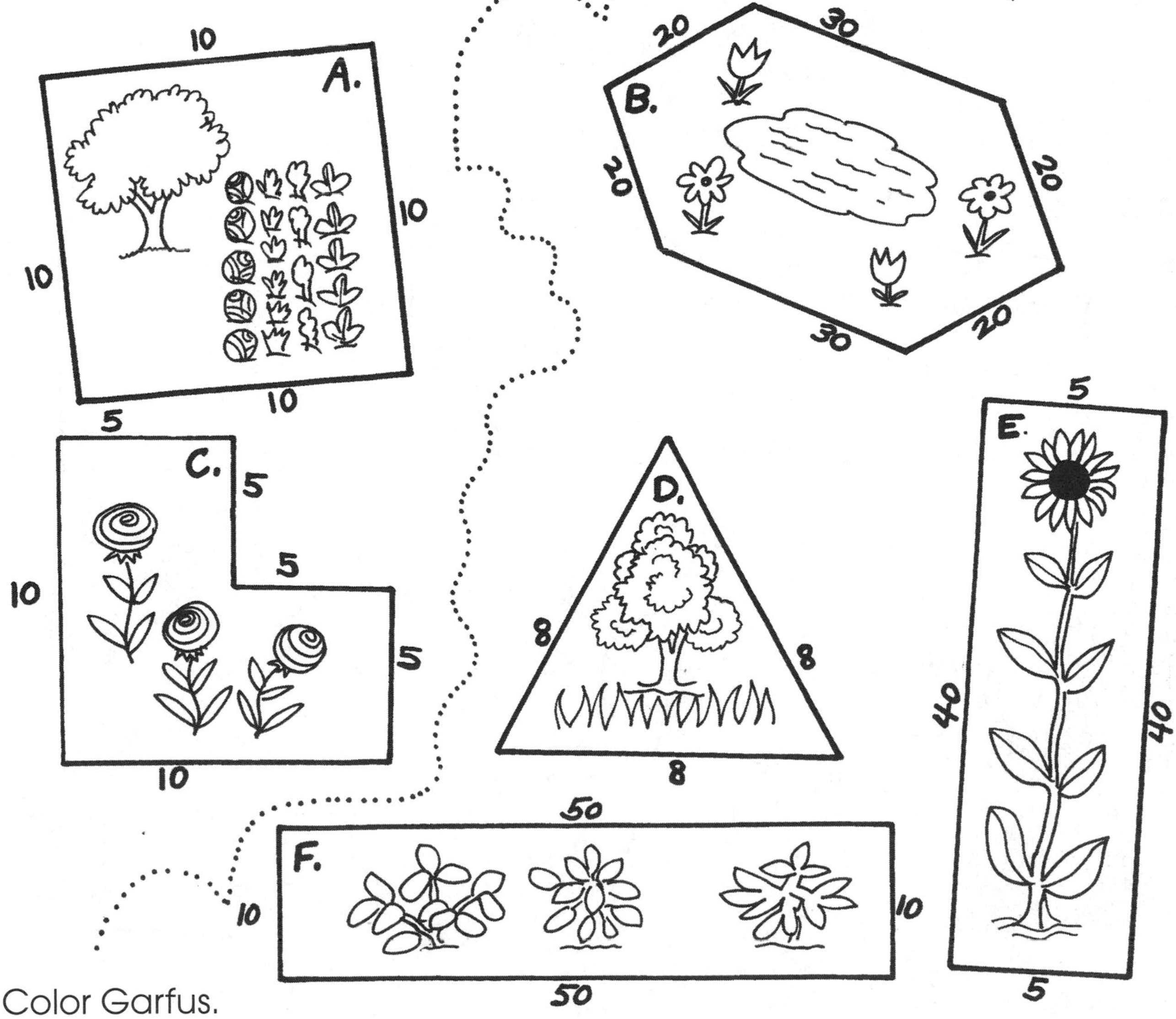

Color Garfus.

Name

Measurement: Perimeter

Around the Edge

School sports take place in all kinds of spaces and places. It seems that practice always starts with the same thing. Kids run around the outside of the field, court, room, or mat!

Figure out how far you would have to run at each of these locations.

Find the perimeter of each shape.
Write P = (the answer) inside each shape.

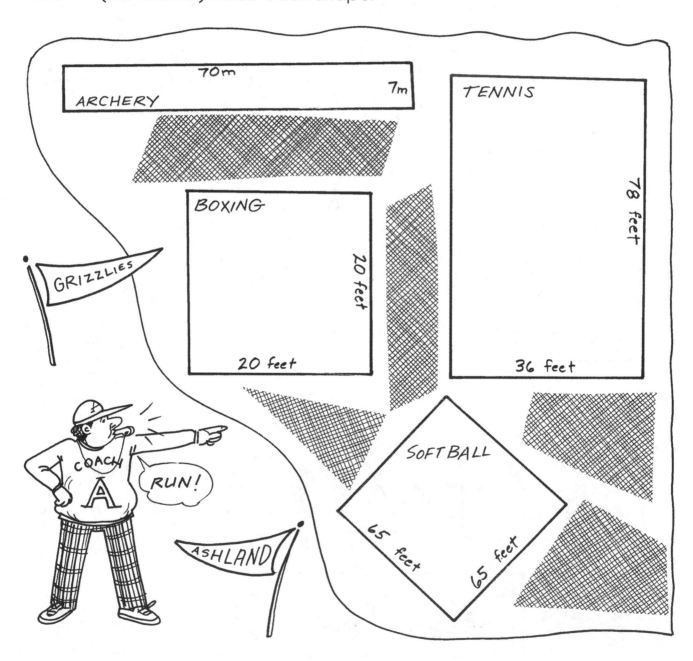

Use with page 109.

Name

Around the Edge, continued

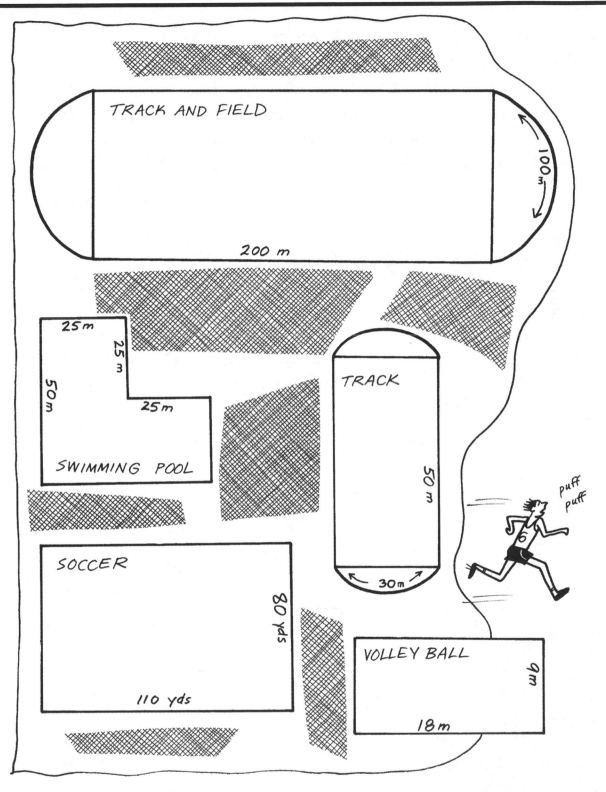

TRACK AND FIELD

100 m

200 m

25 m

25 m

25 m

50 m

25 m

SWIMMING POOL

TRACK

50 m

30 m

puff puff

SOCCER

80 yds

110 yds

VOLLEY BALL

9 m

18 m

How far would you run if you took 10 laps
around the perimeter of the tennis court? _____

Use with page 108.

Name

At the Sports Store

The sports store is one of Joe's favorite spots.

The shelves are full of great stuff for all kinds of sports.

Find the perimeter of each of the items on the shelves.

You can add in your head or work the problems on another piece of paper.

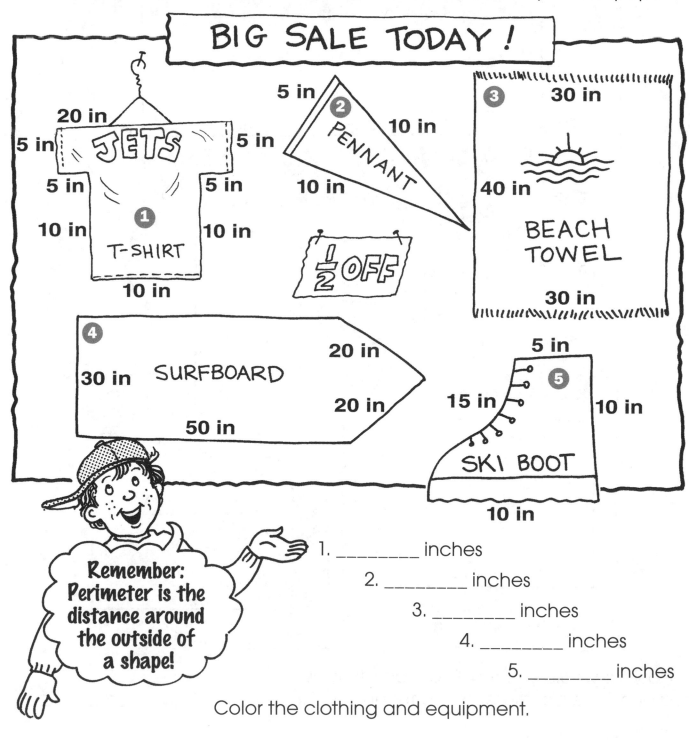

1. _____ inches

2. _____ inches

3. _____ inches

4. _____ inches

5. _____ inches

Color the clothing and equipment.

Name

GEOMETRY

Grade 3

Setting Up Camp

The Turner triplets are off on a long hike.

They set up their campsite by a river. See the picture on page 113.

Their campsite is full of geometric figures.

Follow the directions to find all kinds of points, lines, angles, and figures.

1. Find a point. • Make it green.	6. Here is a circle. Find a circle. Color it orange.
2. Here is a cone. Color 2 cones green.	7. Rectangles have 4 sides. Find a rectangle. Color it pink.
3. These drawings are angles. Find 3 angles. Trace them in red.	8. A square has 4 equal sides. Find a square. Color it purple.
4. Parallel lines do not touch each other. Find a set. Trace them in blue.	9. Line segments are pieces of straight line. Find 5. Trace them in yellow.
5. Here are some curved lines. Find 2 in the picture. Trace them in brown.	10. Triangles have 3 sides. Find 2 triangles. Color them gray.

Use with page 113.

Name

Use with page 112.

Name

Line Up for Cheers

Lines are everywhere! Look all around Sadie to find line segments.

Answer the questions below.

You'll need to do a lot of counting!

A line segment is a part of a **straight** line.

1. How many straight line segments are in Sadie's megaphone? (**Do not** count the letters.) _____ Trace them in red.

2. How many curved lines are in her megaphone? _____ Trace them in black.

3. How many line segments are in Sadie's skirt? _____ Trace them in red.

4. How many line segments are in the H on her megaphone? _____ Trace them in yellow.

5. Are Sadie's streamers made of line segments? _____

6. How many line segments are in the T on her sweater? _____ Trace them in yellow.

7. How many line segments are in the R on her megaphone? _____

Name _____

High-Flying Geometry

Kites would be boring without geometry.

Decorate the kites to show that you know the names of geometric figures.

Color all the hexagons ⬡ blue.

Color all the squares ☐ green.

Color all the triangles △ red or purple.

Color all the rectangles ▭ yellow.

Color all the circles ○ pink.

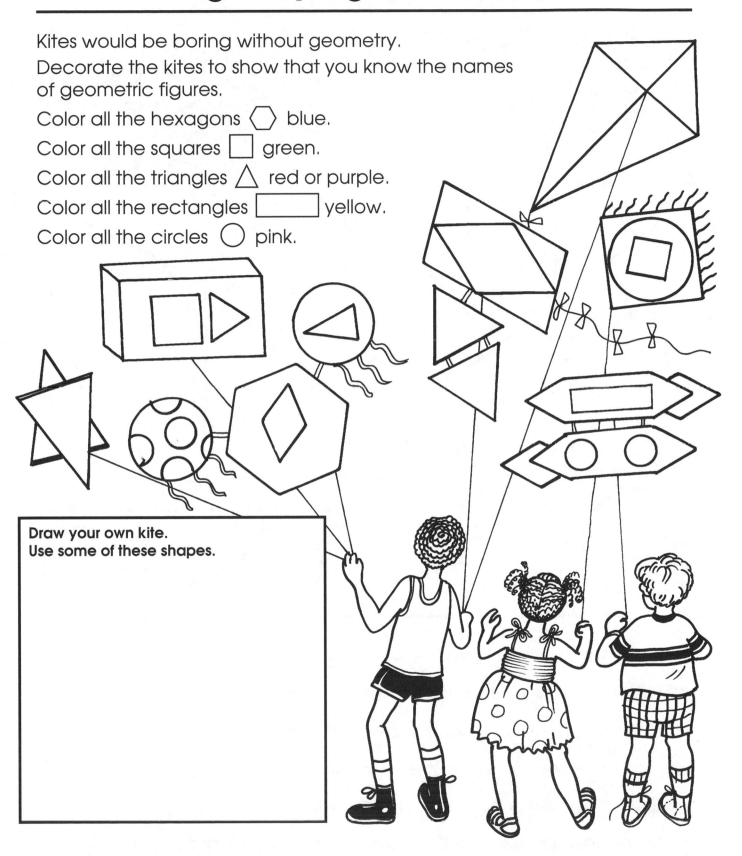

Draw your own kite.
Use some of these shapes.

Name

Shapes and their Attributes

Pool-Bottom Geometry

The painter has just finished painting
a new design on the bottom of the pool.

It is full of different shapes.

Follow the directions to color
the pool bottom.

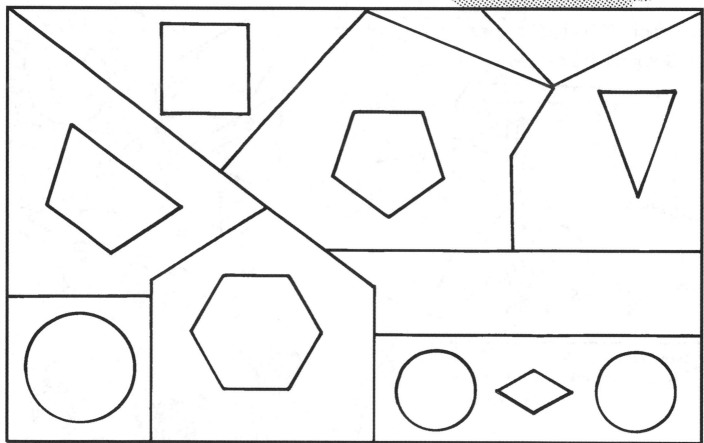

1. Color the triangles green. How many did you find? _____

2. Color the squares blue. How many did you find? _____

3. Draw stripes on the circles. How many did you find? _____

4. Color the pentagons purple. How many did you find? _____

5. Color the hexagons red. How many did you find? _____

6. Color non-square quadrilaterals pink. How many did you find? _____

Name

Flags Everywhere!

Sporting events usually have lots of flags—for countries, states, or teams.
Get a ruler, a compass, and some crayons or markers.
Help Joe, Jana, Joy, and Jon make their flags.
Read the directions to see what to put on each flag.

1.
1 circle
3 triangles
1 rectangle

2.
3 circles
2 line segments

3.
2 angles
4 squares
2 curved lines

4.
6 triangles
1 rectangle
1 circle

Color the flags!

Name

Shapes and their Attributes

In the Bag

Trisha has spilled all these shapes out of her bag.

She wants to compare how they look.

You compare them, too.

A   B   D

C   E

F

G   H   I

J

Write the letters of the shapes from Trisha's bag:

1. quadrilaterals (four sides) _____

2. rectangles _____

3. squares _____

4. trapezoids _____

5. rhombuses _____

Answer the questions.

6. Is C a rectangle?

_____

7. Is a G a quadrilateral?

_____

8. Is F a rhombus?

_____

Name _____

A Wild Bull Ride

These brave cowgirls ride wild bulls in a contest.

They want to see who can stay on a bull longest.

Follow the directions to find out
who won the contest.

1. Draw a square sign for Wanda.   Label it: **Wanda, 2 min., 5 sec.**

2. Draw a rectangle sign for Barb.   Label it: **Barb, 1 min., 50 sec.**

3. Draw a quadrilateral sign for B.J.   Label it: **B.J., 3 min.**

4. Draw a trapezoid sign for Trixie.   Label it: **Trixie, 2 min., 45 sec.**

5. Draw a triangle sign for Cathy.   Label it: **Cathy, 2 min., 13 sec.**

6. What sign shape holds the name of the winner? _____

Name

Shapes and their Attributes

T-Shirt Detectives

This T-shirt detective is looking for shapes on T-shirts. He has come to the right clothesline!

What shape is on each shirt? Write it at the bottom of the shirt.

Write one of these: oval   triangle   square   rectangle

           parallelogram   circle   rhombus   pentagon   trapezoid

Use with page 121.

Name

T-Shirt Detectives, continued

Look at the shape word written on each t-shirt.

Draw a t-shirt design with that shape.

Color your designs on both pages 120 and 121.

J rectangle

K quadrilateral

L pentagon

M rhombus

N square

O oval

P trapezoid

Q circle

R parallelogram

Use with page 120.

Name

Shapes and their Attributes

The Great Shape Match-Up

This basketball team has lots of fans. Each fan holds a card with a shape.

The shapes match words on the players' shirts.

Search the cards. Write the number of a card on the shirt of the matching player.

Name

Different Looks

Ashley is always busy with sports! She has many uniforms and many labels: basketball player, swimmer, soccer player, tennis player, and gymnast.

Quadrilaterals have different looks and different labels, too.

Read these in the box. Write the name of one or more figures to match each description.

1. All sides equal

_____

_____

2. Only one pair of parallel sides

_____

_____

3. Two pairs of equal-length sides

_____

_____

trapezoid   square

quadrilateral

parallelogram

rhombus   rectangle

4. Two pairs of equal-length sides, but no square corners

_____

_____

5. Four sides _____

Write T (true) or F (false) next to each.

_____ 6. All squares
are rectangles.

_____ 7. All rectangles
are quadrilaterals.

_____ 8. All rhombuses
are squares.

_____ 9. A trapezoid is not
a rhombus.

Name

Shapes and their Attributes

The End of the Race

At the end of the race or game, athletes are cold and tired.

Or they might be hot and tired! This is because they have worked hard for a long time indoors, outdoors, or in the water.

Answer the questions on this page and page 125 about their activities today.

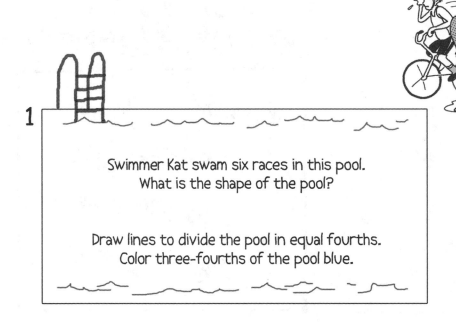

1 Swimmer Kat swam six races in this pool. What is the shape of the pool?

Draw lines to divide the pool in equal fourths. Color three-fourths of the pool blue.

2 Skier Stephan jumped into this ski-bowl today. What is the shape of the bowl?

Draw a line to divide the bowl in half. Color one-half of the bowl yellow.

3 Surfer Amie dried off with this towel. What is its shape?

Draw a line to divide the towel in half. Color two halves pink.

Use with page 125.

Name

The End of the Race, continued

Answer the questions on this page and page 124 about the athletes' activities.

4

Scuba diver Devon walked in this path around a sunken ship 12 times today. What is the shape of the path?

Draw lines to divide the pool in equal halves. Color one-half grey.

5

Suki skated on this ice rink for five hours. What is the shape of the rink?

Draw lines to divide the pool in equal thirds. Color two-thirds silver.

6

Runner Reed ran around this track 25 times. What is the shape?

Draw a line to divide it in thirds. Color one-third red.

7

Biker Brad rode around this track all day. What is its shape?

Draw a line to divide it in half. Color one-half green.

Use with page 124.

Name

Copyright © Incentive Publications
Common Core Reinforcement Activities — 3rd Grade Math

125

Fractional Area

Motorcycle Tracks

These are the different tracks where Julia rides her cycle.

Answer the questions about the tracks.

1. Track area shape is

   _____

2. Fraction of the
   area shaded = _____

3. Track area shape is

   _____

4. Fraction of the
   area shaded = _____

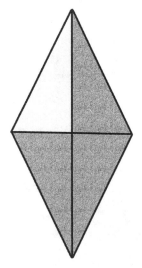

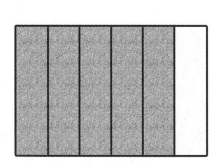

5. Track area shape is

   _____

6. Fraction of the
   area shaded = _____

7. Track area shape is

   _____

8. Fraction of the
   area shaded = _____

Name _____

ASSESSMENT
&
ANSWER KEYS

Math Assessment

PART ONE: OPERATIONS AND ALGEBRAIC THINKING

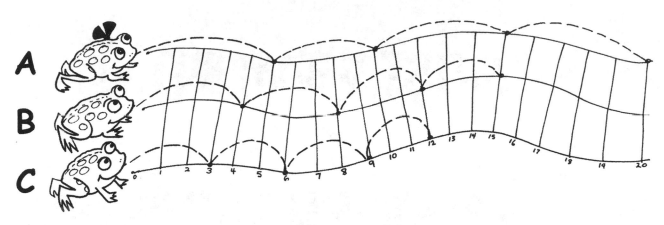

Use the frogs on the number lines to answer questions 1 to 3.

1. Frog A hops 5 spaces 4 times. How far does she hop? _____

2. Frog C hops 3 times for a total of 12 spaces.
   How many spaces does she hop at a time? _____

3. Frog B hops 4 spaces each time for a total
   of 16 hops. How many times does he hop? _____

Write the missing numbers.

4. ☐ x 6 = 18

5. 5 x ☐ = 45

6. 3 x 7 = ☐

7. 10 x ☐ = 80

8. ☐ x 8 = 32

9. 4 x ☐ = 24

10. 5 + 20 = ☐

11. 7 + ☐ = 17

12. 17 – 9 = ☐

13. 13 – 8 = ☐

14. 7 + ☐ = 13

15. 36 ÷ 9 = ☐

Name _____

20.   823
      + 77

21.   500
       − 62

22.   247
      + 605

23.   1000
      − 600

16. The diver sees a group of jellyfish. Which sentence shows the number in the group? (Circle the letter.)
   a. 6 x 5 = 30
   b. 5 x 7 = 35
   c. 5 x 7 = 30

17. Which number sentences are true? (Circle the letters.)
   a. 11 x 7 = 7 x 11
   b. 7 + 11 = 11 + 7
   c. 2 x (3 + 2) = 2 x 5

18. Which number sentences are true? (Circle the letters.)
   a. 20 x 8 = 160
   b. 5 x 8 = 8 x 5
   c. 15 x 1 = 1

19. Which number sentence is NOT true? (Circle the letter.)
   a. 100 ÷ 10 = 10
   b. 12 x 0 = 12
   c. 20 + 0 = 20

24. Julian spins a hula hoop 80 times a minute for 2 minutes. Jojo spins a hula hoop 20 times a minute for 2 minutes. How many more times does Julian spin the hoop than Jojo in the 2 minutes?

_____

25. This frog catches 30 flies a day for 7 days. He gives away 75 flies. He eats the rest. How many flies does he eat?

_____

Name

Assessment

Look at the number on the log.

1. How many hundreds are in this number?

   _____

2. How many tens are in this number?

   _____

Write a number to match the words.

_____ 3. 9 ones and 7 tens

_____ 4. 4 hundreds, 3 tens, and 9 ones

_____ 5. 6 ones and 8 hundreds

_____ 6. 2 thousands and 7 tens

Write the expanded numbers.
Example: 543 = 500 + 40 + 3

7. 416 = _____

8. 7520 = _____

Round to the nearest ten.

9. 79 = _____

10. 243 = _____

Round to the nearest hundred.

11. 629 = _____

12. 486 = _____

Solve the problems.

13.
```
  288
+  99
```

14.
```
   66
   12
+  10
```

15. 7 x 40 = _____

16. 500 x 7 = _____

17. 60 x 8 = _____

18. 900 x 2 = _____

Name

Look at the bugs to answer questions 1, 2, and 3.

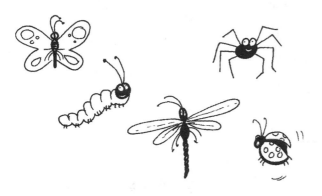

1. What fraction of the critters have spots?

   _____

2. What fraction of the creatures have 8 legs?

   _____

3. What fraction of the creatures have wings?

   _____

4. Write a fraction to show how many thirds of a pizza have NOT been eaten.

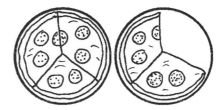

   _____

5. The number line shows a race track from START (0) to FINISH (1). How much of the whole race has Sammy finished? Write a fraction.

   _____

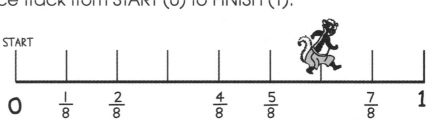

$$\text{START} \quad 0 \quad \frac{1}{8} \quad \frac{2}{8} \quad \frac{4}{8} \quad \frac{5}{8} \quad \frac{7}{8} \quad 1$$

Write >, <, or = to finish each sentence.

6. $\frac{3}{7}$ ☐ $\frac{5}{7}$

7. $\frac{1}{2}$ ☐ $\frac{3}{6}$

8. $\frac{5}{10}$ ☐ $\frac{4}{10}$

9. $\frac{15}{4}$ ☐ $\frac{10}{4}$

10. $\frac{1}{2}$ ☐ $\frac{1}{10}$

11. 1 ☐ $\frac{11}{11}$

Name _____

Assessment

Look at the bug number lines to answer question 12.

12. Which number sentence matches the pair of number lines? (Circle one.)

   a. $\frac{1}{3} = \frac{2}{3}$

   b. $\frac{2}{3} = \frac{4}{6}$

   c. $\frac{1}{2} = \frac{3}{6}$

   d. $\frac{1}{4} = \frac{2}{3}$

If a math statement is true, circle the problem number.

13. $\frac{17}{17} = 1$

14. $\frac{2}{5} + \frac{1}{5} = \frac{3}{5}$

15. $\frac{9}{4} < 1$

16. $\frac{6}{6} = 1$

17. $\frac{5}{9} + \frac{3}{9} = \frac{8}{9}$

18. $\frac{7}{4} < 1$

Use the number line for question 19. Finish writing the fractions to number the line.

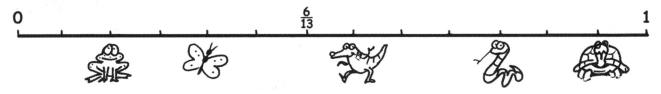

19. How much farther is the snake than the butterfly? Write a fraction. _____

20. What part is checkered? Write a fraction.

21. What part is striped? Write a fraction.

22. What part is flowered? Write a fraction.

Name _____

PART FOUR: MEASUREMENT AND DATA

Write the time that each clock shows.

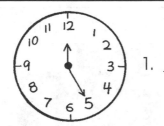 1. _____

 2. _____

3. Which clock shows 6:50?

_____

 A.   B. 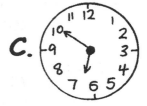   C.

Circle the unit that would be best for measuring each of these.

4. juice in the glass ___ _____   cup   gallon

5. water in the pool _____ _____   pints   gallons

6. weight of cap _____   kilograms   grams

7. weight of weight lifter _____ _____   kilograms   grams

8. weight of bug _____   ounces   pounds

9. height of a building ____ _____   meters   centimeters

Solve the problems.

10. A truck weighs one ton. The driver weighs 97 pounds. What is the total weight of the truck and the driver?

_____

11. Lara drank 3 quarts of water. George drank 3 pints. Who drank the most?

_____

12. Samantha Skunk does pushps for 30 minutes each day. She starts at 1:10 P.M. What time does she finish?

_____

Name _____

Assessment

Use the graph to answer questions 13 through 16.

_____ 13. Which sport has 6 votes?

_____ 14. How many votes are for skating?

_____ 15. Which sport has 1 less vote than swimming?

_____ 16. Which 2 sports got the same number of votes?

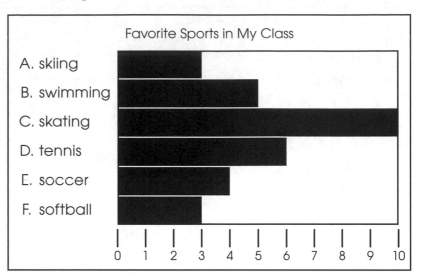

Favorite Sports in My Class

A. skiing
B. swimming
C. skating
D. tennis
E. soccer
F. softball

0 1 2 3 4 5 6 7 8 9 10

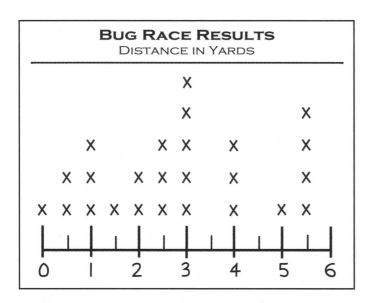

BUG RACE RESULTS
DISTANCE IN YARDS

Use the line plot to answer questions 17 and 18.

17. In a bug race, a ladybug crawled $2\frac{1}{2}$ yards. The line plot shows how far all the racers crawled. How many racers crawled farther than the ladybug?

_____

18. How many bugs crawled 4 yards?

_____

What area does each figure cover? Write the number of square units.

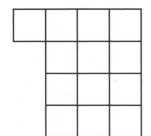

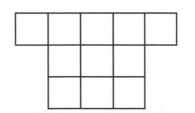

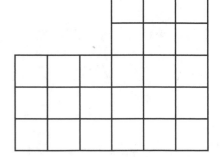

19. _____ 20. _____ 21. _____

Name _____

22. Find the area of the banner.

_____ square inches.

40 IN.

3

9 IN.

Grrrrrrrrrrrrrr

Find the perimeter of each figure. The numbers show the length of each side in inches.

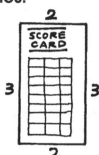

2

SCORE CARD

3   3

2

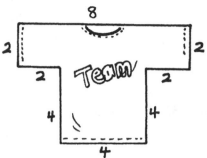

8

2   2

2   2

Team

4   4

4

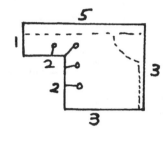

5

1

2

2

3

3

23. _____

24. _____

25. _____

26. A playground is 3 feet wide and 10 feet long. A caterpillar crawled around this playground 5 times. How far did he crawl?

_____

27. A rug is 9 units wide and 20 units long. How much area does it cover?

_____

28. Laranna started a race at 2:10 P.M. It took her 1 hour and 10 minutes. What time did she finish?

_____

29. A swimming pool has a figure on the bottom. It has six equal sides that are each 50 inches long. Jon painted a red line around the figure. How long was the line?

_____

30. A dance team drank a total of 27 Liters of energy drink after rehearsal on Tuesday. On Thursday, they drank 19 Liters less than Tuesday. How much did they drink on Thursday?

_____

Name

Assessment

Write the letter of the figure that matches each term below.

    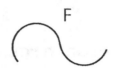 

_____ 1. point

_____ 2. straight line segment

_____ 3. parallel line segments

_____ 4. angle

_____ 5. triangle

_____ 6. curved line segment

Write the letter of the figure that matches each of these:

_____ 7. square

_____ 8. hexagon

_____ 9. triangle

_____ 10. circle

_____ 11. rectangle that is not a square

Write T for True and F for False.

_____ 12. All rectangles are quadrilaterals.

_____ 13. A square is a rhombus.

_____ 14. A square is not a rectangle.

_____ 15. A trapezoid has only two parallel lines.

Name _____

Write the letter of one or more figures to match each of these:

_____ 16. not quadrilateral

_____ 17. 4 sides but not square

_____ 18. rhombus

_____ 19. trapezoid

_____ 20. pentagon

_____ 21. rectangle but not square

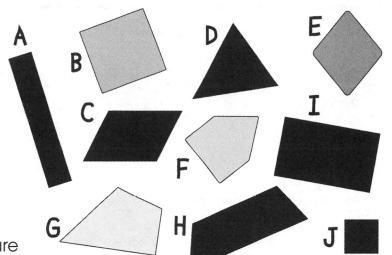

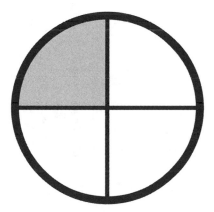

22. What is this shape?

_____

23. What fraction of the shape is NOT shaded?

_____

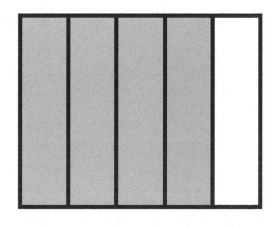

24. What is this shape?

_____

25. What fraction of the shape is NOT shaded?

_____

Name

Assessment

Assessment Answer Key

Part One: Operations and Algebraic Thinking

1. 20 spaces
2. 4
3. 4
4. 3
5. 9
6. 21
7. 8
8. 4
9. 6
10. 25
11. 10
12. 8
13. 5
14. 6
15. 4
16. b
17. a, b, c
18. a, b
19. b
20. 900
21. 438
22. 852
23. 400
24. 120
25. 135

Part Two: Number and Operations in Base Ten

1. 2
2. 0
3. 79
4. 439
5. 806
6. 2070
7. 400 + 10 + 6
8. 7000 + 500 + 20
9. 80
10. 240
11. 600
12. 500
13. 387
14. 88
15. 280
16. 3500
17. 480
18. 1800

Part Three: Number and Operations—Fractions

1. $\frac{2}{5}$
2. $\frac{1}{5}$
3. $\frac{3}{5}$
4. $\frac{5}{3}$
5. $\frac{6}{8}$
6. <
7. =
8. >
9. >
10. >
11. =
12. b
13-18. Circle 13, 14, 16, 17
19. $\frac{6}{13}$ of the way
20. $\frac{3}{5}$
21. $\frac{3}{6}$ or $\frac{1}{2}$
22. $\frac{2}{8}$ or $\frac{1}{4}$

Part Four: Measurement and Data

1. 12:25
2. 4:45
3. C
4. cup
5. gallons
6. grams
7. kilograms
8. ounces
9. meters
10. 2097 pounds
11. Lara
12. 1:40 P.M.
13. D (tennis)
14. 10
15. E (soccer)
16. A (skiing) and F (softball)
17. 13
18. 3
19. 13
20. 11
21. 27
22. 360 square inches
23. 10 inches
24. 28 inches
25. 16 inches
26. 130 ft
27. 180 square units
28. 3:20 P.M.
29. 300 inches
30. 8 L

Part Five: Geometry

1. B
2. C
3. A
4. E
5. D
6. F
7. E
8. F
9. B
10. A
11. C
12. T
13. T
14. F
15. T
16. D, F
17. A, C, E, G, H, I
18. B, E, J
19. H
20. F
21. A, I
22. circle
23. $\frac{3}{4}$
24. rectangle
25. $\frac{1}{5}$

Copyright © Incentive Publications
Common Core Reinforcement Activities — 3rd Grade Math

Activities Answer Key

Operations and Algebraic Thinking (pages 18–42)

pages 18–19
1. 2
2. 2
3. 3
4. 3
5. 1
6. 2
7. 1; 5
8. 2
9. 1

page 20
Race 1: 15, 16, 18, Gus

Race 2: 30, 24, 9, Frannie

Race 3: 10, 12, 12, Robbie and Gus tie

Race 4: 15, 4, 6, Frannie

Race 5: 25, 16, 9, Frannie

Race 6: 10, 12, 6, Robbie

page 21
1. 8
2. 9
3. 27
4. 16
5. 9
6. 8
7. 4
8. 9
9. 8
10. 5
11. 12
12. 49

page 22
1. 9
2. 9
3. 5
4. 6
5. 3
6. 8

page 23
1. 4 x 5 = 20
2. 4 x 5 = 20
3. 9 x 2 = 18
4. 3 x 7 = 21
5. 5 x 7 = 35
   OR
   7 x 5 = 35
6. 6 x 8 = 48
   OR
   8 x 6 = 48

page 24
1. Rick; 3, 18
2. surfer; 72, 9
3. Chen; 10, 50
4. Jean; 40, 20
5. George; 11, 88

page 25
Jan, 24
June, 27
Julie, 100
Jamie, 8
Jerri, 8
James, 6
Janet, 9
Jenny, 9
John, 5
Justin, 5

page 26
Across
1. 48
4. 2000
5. 420
7. 56
8. 40
9. 303
11. 35
13. 50
14. 32
16. 30
17. 72
Down
1. 444
2. 6000
3. 5555
4. 200
6. 24
9. 300
10. 36
11. 333
12. 777
13. 500
15. 27

page 27
1. 90
2. 9
3. 18
4. 10
5. 10
6. 81
7. 6
8. 1000
9. 9

page 28
1. x
2. x
3. x
4. x
5. ÷
6. ÷
7. x
8. x
9. ÷
10. ÷
11. x
12. ÷
13. x
14. x
15. x
16. ÷
17. x
18. ÷
19. ÷
20. ÷

page 29
1. 4
2. 4
3. 7
4. 5
5. 10
6. 25
7. 10
8. 25
9. 1
10. 2
11. 8
12. 18
13. 9
14. 9

page 30
1. 16 (each number is twice the previous number)
2. 2, 2 (each number is the previous number multiplied by 1 or divided by 1)
3. 7 (subtract 4)
4. 12 (add 1, add 2, add 3, add 4, and so on)
5. 11 (each is the previous number divided by 2)

page 31
1. 9, yellow
2. 10, orange
3. 4, silver
4. 11, gold
5. 7, blue
6. 9, yellow
7. 6, purple
8. 4, silver
9. 6, purple
10. 5, green
11. 4, silver
12. 8, red

page 32
1. 12, 6
2. 36, 9
3. 9, 45
4. 54, 54
5. 8, 6
6. 4, 3
7. 4, 20
8. 49, 7
9. 11, 11

page 33
1. 984, I
2. 1336, T
3. 1092, S
4. 981, E
5. 2166, A
6. 1632, W
7. 1632, W
8. 952, H
9. 952, H
10. 934, N
Shawn White, Olympic snowboarder

page 34
Game A, a winner!
Row 1: 11, 11, 10
Row 2: 9, 8, 9
Row 3: 11, 10, 10

Game B, a winner!
Row 1: 6, 9, 6
Row 2: 22, 7, 22
Row 3: 8, 4, 8

Game C, not a winner.
Row 1: 20, 9, 9
Row 2: 10, 5, 5
Row 3: 9, 10, 9

page 35
Boulders: 40;
Danger Drop Rapids: 5;
Terror Corner: 15;
Log Jam: 18;
Fearsome Falls: 9;
Powerhouse Dam: 36;
Whirlpool: 6;
Lazy Ripples: 12;
Picnic Cove: 30;
Home Base: 10.
Answer is 10.

pages 36–37
1. $115.42
2. $10.05
3. stick, $3.58 less
4. yes
5. $38.00
6. elbow pads and a stick
7. $139.95
8. $34.43
9. $105.93
10. $35.00

page 38
1. Cost .75, Change .25
2. Cost 1.25, Change .75
3. Cost .20, Change .30
4. Cost .85, Change .15
5. Cost 1.60, Change .40
6. Cost 1.50, Change 3.50
7. Cost .25, Change .25
8. Cost 1.00, Change 4.00

page 39
1. 81
2. 15 cents
3. 5
4. 48
5. 20
6. 25

page 40
1. 10 dollars
2. 4
3. 11
4. 46
5. no
6. yes
7. no
8. no

page 41
1. 70
2. 16
3. 200
4. add six miles each day
5. subtract 400 strokes each hour
6. no

page 42
1. T
2. T
3. F
4. T
5. T
6. F
7. F
8. T
9. F
10. T
11. T
12. F
13. Add 600 each day

Activities Answer Key

page 44
1. 3265
2. 6261
3. 2359
4. 8045
5. 6372
6. 6421
7. 1070

page 45
1. 30; 60; 430; 5780; 670; 710; 5500
2. 130; 60; 280; 7780; 200; 990; 9260
3. 100; 200; 400; 3400; 800; 300; 1500
4. 100; 500; 900; 2600; 800; 5700
5. 1000; 16,000; 7000; 88,000

page 46
1. 4263
2. 1810
3. 9246
4. 7221
5. 231
6. 5202
7. 300 + 20 + 9
8. 600 + 70 + 8
9. 500 + 90
10. 1000 + 500 + 70 + 2
11. 4000 + 400 + 70 + 7
12. 2000 + 800 + 30 + 1

page 47
A. correct ....(Color.)
B. 832 .... (Do not color.)
C. 1400 ....(Do not color.)
D. correct ....(Color.)
E. 402 .... (Do not color.)
F. correct ....(Color.)
G. correct ....(Color.)
H. 9001 .... (Do not color.)
I. correct ....(Color.)
J. correct ....(Color.)
K. 69 .... (Do not color.)
L. correct ....(Color.)

page 48
1. 280
2. 50
3. 3560
4. 3400
5. 70
6. 100
7. 510
8. 280
9. 1030
10. 990

page 49
Across
A. 89
B. 746
E. 3555
G. 4002
H. 5736
J. 2109
L. 9870
N. 135
Down
A. 8665
C. 6032
D. 90,007
F. 5702
I. 620
J. 2483
K. 99
M. 7170
N. 16

page 50
Lost sports equipment is hockey stick. Examine colored picture for sensible coloring. Hockey stick is yellow. Snake is black and blue stripes, frog is green, chicken is brown, ladybug is red and black. Background colors are purple and orange.

page 51
Correct answers are numbers 1, 2, 5, 7, 8, 10. These lassos should be colored.

page 52
Highest score of games 1, 2, or 3 is Game 3—50.
Game 1. 38
Game 2. 43
Game 3. 50
Game 4. 29
Game 5. 50
Game 6. 27
Game 7. 68
Game 8. 46
Game 9. 15
Game 10. 38
Game 11. 40

page 53
1. 22
2. 9
3. 25
4. 2491
5. 14
6. 26
7. 5

8. 16
9. 300
10. 21
11. 54
12. 4
13. 400

page 54
1. 92; yellow
2. 32; blue
3. 177; red
4. 35; blue
5. 86; yellow
6. 35; blue
7. 50; striped
8. 123; red
9. 49; blue
10. 76; yellow

page 55
1. 473
2. 954
3. 227
4. 106
5. 688
6. 29
7. 372
8. 33
9. 888
10. 172

page 56
Kerry had the most right answers.
Terry: Answers A and C are wrong.
A: 114; C: 120
Kerry: Answer E is wrong: 791
Mary: Answers J and L are wrong.
J: 16; L: 481
Barry: Answers N and O are wrong.
N: 395; O: 275

page 57
1. 720
2. 250
3. 420
4. 80
5. 320
6. 48
7. 2000
8. 360

page 58
Examine picture for sensible coloring. Pictures should reveal green leaves and forest background, an upside-down brown bat, a black bear, an upside-down black bat, a pink rabbit, an upside-down yellow deer, and orange glow around the campers at the fire.

page 60
1. 4/6 or 2/3
2. 3/6 or 1/2
3. 2/6 or 1/3
4. 1/6
5. 1/6
6. 5/12
7. 3/12 or 1/4
8. 2/12 or 1/6
9. 2/3
10. 1/2
11. 1/4
12. 2/4 or 1/2
13. 1/4
14. 2/3

page 61
1. 3/6 or 1/2
2. 5/12
3. 1/6
4. 5/6
5. 2/6 or 1/3
6. 2/12 or 1/6
7. 1/6
8. 4/6 or 2/3
9. 2/6 or 1/3
10. 1/6

page 62
1. Rocky ate 1 1/4
2. Ernest ate 1 2/3
3. Bruiser ate 2 5/6
4. Jess ate 1 1/2
5. Kujo ate 2 3/4
6. Bud ate 1 5/6
Bruiser ate the most.
Rocky left the most.

page 63
1. E
2. C
3. F
4. H
5. B
6. L
7. D
8. B
9. M
10. G
11. J
12. I
13. F
14. B
15. M
16. L

page 64
1-5: Check to see that correct amounts are colored.
6. 2 2/4 or 2 1/2
7. 1 9/12 or 1 3/4

page 65
1. 6/8
2. 5/6
3. Check for skunk drawn at 3/5 on number line.
4. Check to see that skunks are drawn at 3/10, 6/10, and 9/10.

page 66
Check to see that number lines are correctly numbered with fractions.
1. Bosco
2. Bee
3. Bob
4. Babs

page 67
1. Check to see that red ball is drawn at 1/4.
2. Check to see that blue ball is drawn at 1/8.
3. Check to see that green ball is drawn at 1/6.
4. Check to see that orange ball is drawn at 1/2.

page 68
1. 1/2 and 2/4
2. 2/3 and 4/6
3. 1/2 and 3/6
4. 3/4 and 6/8

page 69
1. #2
2. #3 and #4
3. #1, #6, #7

page 70
1. 2/4
2. 2/3
3. 1/3
4. 1/4
5. 1/2
6. 4/8

page 71
1. 1/3
2. 4/8; 2/4
3. 6/9
4. 3/4
5. 4/10
6. 1/5
7. 1/4 and 2/8
8. 4/5 and 8/10

page 72
1. c
2. d
3. a
4. b
5. c
6. c

page 73
1. 10 4/5 (rock)
2. 5 3/4 (stump)
3. 3 1/4 (stump with owl)
4. 2/4 (umbrella)
5. 3/3 (frog in boat); 15/15 (rock); 4/4 (bunny on float); 8/8 (log)
6. 5 6/10 (tree)
7. 10/2 (rock)
8. 2 2/4 (beaver house)
9. 2 2/3 (rock under tree)
10. 5 3/4 (stump)
11. 2/4 (umbrella)

page 74
1. 1
2. 1
3. 1
4. 4
5. 7
6. 10
7. 10
8. 1
9. 6
10. 1
11. 1
12. 1

page 75
1. blue: 8/10 and 40/50
2. red: 3/12 and 2/8

3. purple: 5/5; 13/13; 20/20; 12/12; 7/7; 7/7
4. green: 2/7
5. yellow: 2/5 and 8/20
6. brown: 3/9
7. pink: 5/10; 2/4; 3/6; 4/8; 10/20, 6/12
8. no

page 76
1. 6/8
2. 6/4
3. 1 1/4
4. 15/3
5. >
6. =
7. <
8. <
9. >
10. >
11. =
12. =

page 77
A. no
B. more
C. Freddy
D. 7/9
E. no
F. 22 3/4
G. more
H. singers

page 78
A. >
B. =
C. >
D. <
E. =
F. =
G. >
H. <
I. >
J. =
K. >
L. =
M. =

page 80
1. no
2. yes
3. no
4. no
5. yes
6. no
7. yes
8. yes

page 81
Check clocks to see that times have been shown accurately.
1. 11:30
2. 2:50
3. 3:50
4. 1:00
5. 8:10
6. 9:40
7. 10:45
8. 4:35

pages 82–83
1. yes
2. yes
3. 100-Yard Potato Sack Hop; Softball Throw
4. Lunch, Bubblegum-Blowing, or Frisbee
5. 30
6. 12:00 P.M.
7. 2 hours, 15 minutes (or 2 1/4 hours)
8. 1 hour, 30 minutes (or 1 1/2 hours)
9. late
10. 4 P.M. or later

page 84
Discuss these answers with students. Listen to students' ideas, conclusions, and questions about the measurements. Answers and reasons for them may vary.
1. gallons
2. gallons
3. gallons
4. gallons
5. cups
6. gallons

page 85
Discuss these answers with students. Listen to students' ideas, conclusions, and questions about the measurements. Answers and reasons for them may vary.
1. 1/4 L
2. 1 L
3. 20 L
4. 300 L
5. 7 L
6. 10,000 L
7. 300 L
8. 5000 L

page 86
Discuss these answers with students. Listen to students' ideas, conclusions, and questions about the measurements. Answers and reasons for them may vary.
1. lb or t
2. lb
3. oz
4. lb
5. oz
6. lb
7. oz
8. t
9. oz
10. lb
11. 4 pounds
12. 1050 pounds

page 87
Discuss these answers with students. Listen to students' ideas, conclusions, and questions about the measurements. Answers and reasons for them may vary.
1. g
2. g
3. g
4. kg
5. kg
6. g
7. g
8. kg
9. kg
10. g
11. kg
12. kg
13. g
14. g

page 88–89
1. 15 seconds
2. 28 pounds
3. 15, warmer
4. 16
5. 1 foot, 4 inches or 16 in
6. 5
7. 30

page 90
1. Frost-Tea
2. 13
3. 3
4. 1
5. Quick-Gulp and Slug-Ade
6. 1
7. 6
8. Slug-Ade

page 91
1. Jumping Jake
2. Tuesday
3. 36
4. 16 feet
5. Thursday
6. Wednesday and Friday
7. Jumping Jake and Tilly Toad
8. Jumping Jake
9. Monday and Tuesday

page 92
1. 12
2. bruises
3. 2
4. 14
5. black eyes
6. frost bite
7. 10
8. 20
9. broken bones
10. 4

page 93
Check student graphs to see that bars have been colored accurately.

page 94
Measurements may vary slightly due to shrinkage of images upon copying. Answers below may vary by a centimeter.
1. 6
2. 7
3. 6
4. 6

5. 9
6. 5
7. 10

page 95
Measurements may vary slightly due to shrinkage of images upon copying. Answers below may vary by a quarter inch.
1. 3 1/4 inches
2. 4 1/4 inches
3. 2 1/2 inches
4. 4 3/4 inches
5. 2 1/2 inches
6. 4 inches

page 96
Discuss these answers with students. Listen to students' ideas, conclusions, and questions about the measurements. Answers and reasons for them may vary.
1. feet
2. miles
3. inches (or feet)
4. inches
5. inches
6. feet
7. inches
8. inches
9. inches
10. feet
11. feet
12. feet

page 97
Answers will vary. Observe students as they measure, and check reasonableness of answers.

page 98
1. 2
2. 11
3. 2
4. 0
Check Line Plot B to see that there are the following number of x's at each location on plot:
0 - 1
1/2 - none
1 - none
1 1/2 - 1

2 - none
2 1/2 - 1
3 - 2
3 1/2 - 1
4 - none
4 1/2 - 2
5 - 2
5 1/2 - none
6 - 2

page 99
Answers are approximations and may vary. Discuss with students how they arrived at answers.
1. 2
2. 7
3. 2
4. 8
5. 12 or 13
6. 12
7. 54
Josie: 27-28

pages 100–101
1. 4
2. 4
3. 9
4. 12
5. 2
6. 2
7. 6
8. 4 (or 3)
9. 8
10. 2

page 102
1. 14
2. 12
3. 18
4. 11
5. 28
6. 27
7. 3
8. trampoline
9. diving board
10. t-shirt
11. no

page 103
1. 100 in
2. 16 ft
3. 18 ft
4. 240 in
5. 22 ft
6. 240 cm
7. 34 ft
8. 9 yds

page 104
1. 58 in
2. 10 ft
3. 136 in
4. 96 in
5. 6 1/2 ft
6. 120 in
7. 60 in
8. #7

page 105
1. SALE sign
2. Ping Pong Balls
3. Pom Poms
4. Hockey Sticks
5. Ping Pong Balls
6. Tennis Shoes
7. 25 square units

page 106
1. 6 square units
2. bed
3. 8 square units
4. 20 square units
5. 3 square units
6. 3 square units
7. no

page 107
!. 40
B. 140
C. 40
D. 24
E. 90
F. 120

pages 108–109
Archery:.......P = 154 m
Tennis:..........P = 228 feet
Boxing:.........P = 80 feet
Softball:.......P = 260 feet
Track and
   Field:........P = 600 m
Swimming
   Pool: ....P = 200 m
Track:...........P = 160 m
Soccer: ....P = 380 yds
Volleyball:....P = 54 m

Ten laps around the tennis court = 2280 ft.

page 110
1. 70
2. 25
3. 140
4. 170
5. 40

Activities Answer Key

pages 112–113
Check student work to see that directions have been followed accurately.

page 114
Discuss work with students. Review what a line segment is and distinguish between straight and curved line segments. When students are counting segments, answers may vary, depending upon where they think the segment starts and stops (for example, letters for #4 and #6)
1. 2
2. 2
3. 9
4. 3 or 5
5. yes—curved line segments
6. 2 or 3
7. 4

page 115
Check coloring to see that students have identified shapes correctly.

page 116
1. 4
2. 2
3. 3
4. 5
5. 2
6. 3, or 4 if you count the pool edge

page 117
Check to see that flags have required elements.

page 118
1. A, B, C, E, G, H, I, J
2. A, B, I, J
3. B, J
4. H
5. B, E, J
6. no
7. yes
8. no

page 119
1-5. Examine student drawings for accuracy.
6. quadrilateral (Student may give it other names, depending on whether the quadrilateral drawn is a rhombus, a rectangle, a square, a parallelogram, or other quadrilateral.)

pages 120–121
A. circle
B. square, rectangle, rhombus, or parallelogram
C. rectangle or parallelogram
D. pentagon
E. triangle
F. parallelogram
G. trapezoid
H. oval
I. rhombus
J-R. Check drawings to see that they match labels.

page 122
Answers may vary. Other than answers below, students may connect Rae to the rectangle (1) or the square (6).
Pam may be labeled rectangle (1), square (6), rhombus/diamond (9) or parallelogram (10).
1. Rae
2. Tru
3. Helen
4. Tish
5. Dee
6. Suki
7. Olive
8. Pat
9. Rosa
10. Pam

page 123
1. square or rhombus
2. trapezoid
3. rectangle, rhombus, or parallelogram
4. parallelogram or trapezoid
5. quadrilateral
6. T
7. T
8. F
9. T

pages 124–125
1. rectangle; check coloring to see that it shows 3/4 blue
2. oval; check coloring to see that it shows 1/2 yellow
3. square; check coloring to see that it shows 2 halves pink
4. pentagon; check coloring to see that it shows 1/2 grey
5. rectangle; check coloring to see that it shows 2/3 silver
6. triangle; check coloring to see that it shows 1/3 red
7. trapezoid; check coloring to see that it shows 1/2 green.

page 126
1. oval
2. 1/4
3. triangle
4. 1 or 4/4
5. rhombus
6. 3/4
7. rectangle or parallelogram
8. 5/6